CAMPAIGN 343

PETSAMO AND KIRKENES 1944

The Soviet offensive in the Northern Arctic

DAVID GREENTREE   ILLUSTRATED BY GRAHAM TURNER

Series editor Marcus Cowper

OSPREY PUBLISHING
Bloomsbury Publishing Plc
PO Box 883, Oxford, OX1 9PL, UK
1385 Broadway, 5th Floor, New York, NY 10018, USA
E-mail: info@ospreypublishing.com
www.ospreypublishing.com

OSPREY is a trademark of Osprey Publishing Ltd

First published in Great Britain in 2019

A catalogue record for this book is available from the British Library.

ISBN: PB: 978 1 4728 3113 2
          ePub: 978 1 4728 3114 9
          ePDF: 978 1 4728 3115 6
          XML: 978 1 4728 3116 3

19 20 21 22 23   10 9 8 7 6 5 4 3 2 1

Index by Nick Hayhurst
Typeset in Myriad Pro and Sabon
Maps by Bounford.com
3D BEVs by The Black Spot
Page layouts by PDQ Digital Media Solutions, Bungay, UK
Printed and bound in India by Replika Press Private Ltd.

Artist's note

Readers may care to note that the original paintings from which the colour
plates in this book were prepared are available for private sale. All
reproduction copyright whatsoever is retained by the Publishers. Readers
are directed to the following website for further information:
www.studio88.co.uk
The Publishers regret that they can enter into no correspondence upon
this matter.

Osprey Publishing supports the Woodland Trust, the UK's leading woodland
conservation charity.

To find out more about our authors and books visit
www.ospreypublishing.com. Here you will find extracts, author
interviews, details of forthcoming events and the option to sign up for
our newsletter.

Author's acknowledgements

I would like to thank Major James F. Gebhardt, US Army (Retd.) for his
involvement with the research for this book. Without his assistance I would
not have had access to the various Soviet sources he has compiled over the
years. His ability to translate official Soviet reports, the personal reminisces
of participants and the work of Soviet historians assisted me immensely.
His knowledge of the Cape Krestovyi attack in particular cleared up
uncertainties and his tactical insight added to my understanding. Simon
Orchard generously provided me with the official reports that provide
much of the German tactical detail in the book. I would like to express my
gratitude to my uncle, Colin Greentree, and my neighbour, Marcus Leier, for
translating those that I needed.

Finnish suffix meanings

-järvi	lake
-joki	river
-mäki	hill
-niemi	peninsula, headland
-tunturi	mountain fell
-vuono	fjord

Key to military symbols

Army Group	Army	Corps	Division	Brigade	Regiment	Battalion
Company/Battery	Platoon	Section	Squad	Infantry	Artillery	Cavalry
Airborne	Unit HQ	Air defence	Air Force	Air mobile	Air transportable	Amphibious
Anti-tank	Armour	Air aviation	Bridging	Engineer	Headquarters	Maintenance
Medical	Missile	Mountain	Navy	Nuclear, biological, chemical	Ordnance	Parachute
Reconnaissance	Signal	Supply	Transport movement	Rocket artillery	Air defence artillery	

Key to unit identification

Unit Identifier / Parent unit
Commander
(+) with added elements
(–) less elements

PREVIOUS PAGE
Soviet infantry move forward.

CONTENTS

Soviet offensive to capture Petsamo and Kirkenes, phases 1 and 2: 7–23 October 1944

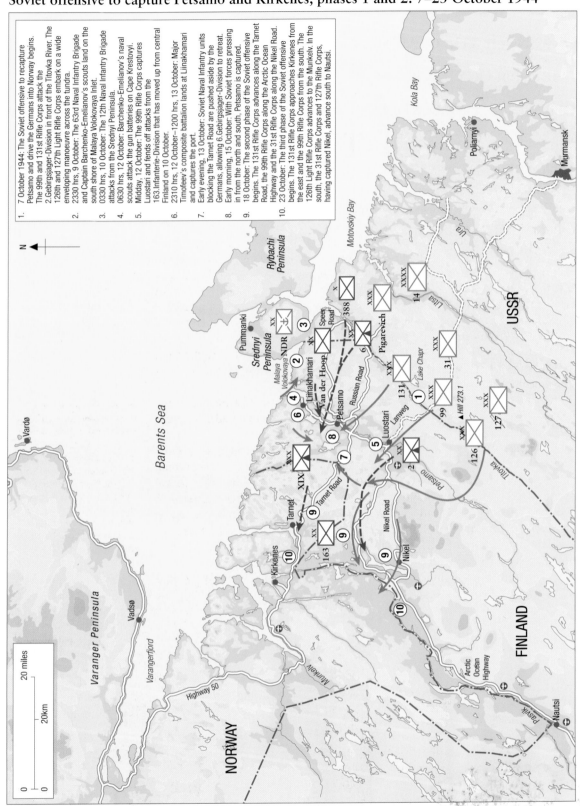

1. 7 October 1944: The Soviet offensive to recapture Petsamo and drive the Germans into Norway begins. The 99th and 131st Rifle Corps attack the 2.Gebirgsjäger-Division in front of the Titovka River. The 126th and 127th Light Rifle Corps embark on a wide enveloping manoeuvre across the tundra.
2. 2330 hrs, 9 October: The 63rd Naval Infantry Brigade and Captain Barchenko-Emelianov's scouts land on the south shore of Malaya Volokovaya Inlet.
3. 0330 hrs, 10 October: The 12th Naval Infantry Brigade attacks from the Srednyi Peninsula.
4. 0630 hrs, 12 October: Barchenko-Emelianov's naval scouts attack the gun batteries on Cape Krestovyi.
5. Midday, 12 October: The 99th Rifle Corps captures Luostari and fends off attacks from the 163.Infanterie-Division that has moved up from central Finland on 10 October.
6. 2310 hrs, 12 October–1200 hrs, 13 October: Major Timofeev's composite battalion lands at Liinakhamari and captures the port.
7. Early evening, 13 October: Soviet Naval Infantry units blocking the Tarnet Road are pushed aside by the Germans, allowing 6.Gebirgsjäger-Division to retreat.
8. Early morning, 15 October: With Soviet forces pressing in from the north and south, Petsamo is captured.
9. 18 October: The second phase of the Soviet offensive begins. The 131st Rifle Corps advances along the Tarnet Road, the 99th Rifle Corps along the Arctic Ocean Highway and the 31st Rifle Corps along the Nikel Road.
10. 23 October: The third phase of the Soviet offensive begins. The 131st Rifle Corps approaches Kirkenes from the east and the 99th Rifle Corps from the south. The 126th Light Rifle Corps advances to the Munkelv. In the south, the 31st Rifle Corps and 127th Rifle Corps, having captured Nikel, advance south to Nautsi.

ORIGINS OF THE CAMPAIGN

On 7 October 1944, 97,000 men of the Soviet Karelian Front commanded by General Kirill Meretskov launched an offensive against 56,000 Germans of XIX.Gebirgs-Korps commanded by General der Gebirgstruppe Ferdinand Jodl to capture the Finnish town of Petsamo and the Norwegian port of Kirkenes. Earlier that summer, two offensives – north of Leningrad and in southern Karelia – had forced the Finnish government to sign an armistice on 4 September that provided for the expulsion of German forces from their country by 15 September. On 3 October, Hitler had sanctioned a withdrawal from central Finland to Ivalo and Rovaniemi prior to a further move into northern Norway. The forces near Petsamo would be withdrawn too; however, the Germans wanted to hold their positions until supplies could be evacuated.

Hitler had realized the importance of the harbour at Murmansk to the Soviet war effort, and in June 1941, the Germans had attempted to capture the ice-free port and interdict the railway from Murmansk to Leningrad. The advance was halted in September along the Litsa River, where the Germans built strong defensive positions. The continued presence of German forces in the area was strategically important to their war effort. The nickel mines at Koloszoki (Nikel) and the iron ore mines near Kirkenes needed to be protected from Soviet attack. Also, the air and naval bases in the region were used to interdict Allied convoys bringing in supplies across the Barents Sea. By late 1944, the ability to interdict these convoys was limited and the Germans no longer needed to hold onto the nickel mines. In three years, German engineers had extracted 10,000 tons of nickel ore annually for weapons production; Albert Speer, the armaments minister, assured Hitler that, with two years' worth of stockpiles, Germany no longer needed the mines.

The desolate landscape around Petsamo and Kirkenes was described by the commander of German forces sent there in 1941 – Generaloberst Edward Dietl

The Northern Arctic was a bleak prospect for many Soviet recruits. There were two army divisions that spent the entire war here: 10th Guards Rifle Division, and 14th Rifle Division. Most troops were brought in from further south. Here, a Soviet army patrol is seen in 1941 on the shores of the Barents Sea. (TASS via Getty Images)

The initial advance to the Litsa River in the summer of 1941 was through barren terrain on dirt roads that, when the rains occurred in September, were of practically no use. (Ullstein Bild via Getty Images)

The building of roads was critical to maintaining the German Army, which was unable to obtain anything from the land. Here, workers of the Organisation Todt are building a new road in the northern Arctic. (Ullstein Bild via Getty Images)

– as not supportive of military operations. Situated 320km north of the Arctic Circle near the Barents coast, Petsamo was the main settlement in the region that was ceded to the Soviet Union following the 1940 Winter War with Finland. In October, when the Soviets launched their offensive, the climate was cold and moist with temperatures of between plus and minus 5 degrees. Frequent precipitation fell either as snow, or mixed rain and snow. Heavy fog often descended from the Barents. Daylight hours reduced from 13.5 to 10 at the end of the month. Inland hills covered with rock and ascending to 580m could be covered with snow. The Soviets had to move and fight through many gullies, ravines, bogs and marshes, and low scrub trees and bushes offered further obstacles to movement and assisted the defenders in restricting the avenues the attackers could use.

The Germans relied on Highway 50 as the main supply route along the Norwegian coast to Kirkenes. A secondary road went from Kirkenes to Tarnet, and from here the Germans had extended the road to Petsamo. Spurs went further east to Titovka (Speer Road) and south to the Litsa River (Russian Road) where positions were occupied by 6.Gebirgs-Division with Grenadier-Brigade 388 attached. Another main road originating from Rovaniemi, the Arctic Ocean Highway, went north through Salmijärvi, Nikel, Luostari, Petsamo and on to the port of Liinakhamari. At Luostari, a secondary road (the Lanweg) led to the Titovka River, where positions were occupied by 2.Gebirgs-Division in front and behind the river from Lake Chapr (Tschapr See) to Hill 237.1. Further inland, the terrain was thought to be unsuitable for military operations and no defences existed.

The Soviets used a single road from Murmansk, though other lateral roads were being built in the summer. No road yet linked the Soviet and German positions. The building of roads to join up with the German network would be given priority. The Soviet preparations went largely undetected; however, Generalleutnant Hans Degen, the commander of 2.Gebirgs-Division, fully expected a Soviet offensive, and in September issued a proclamation to his soldiers that stated the attackers would be permitted to hurl themselves against their strongly prepared strongpoints before being destroyed by a counter-attack. His divisional order correctly identified that the focus of the Soviet attack would be along the Lanweg.

CHRONOLOGY

1944

7–8 October
Soviets launch the Petsamo and Kirkenes Offensive at 0800 hrs on 7 October. 131st Rifle Corps reaches the Titovka south of the Laja See by the evening, but 99th Rifle Corps crosses the river only late the following day.

Evening, 8 October
Rendulic, worried about the Soviets breaking through, gives permission for a move from the Titovka River to Luostari by 2.Gebirgs-Division. He authorizes Jodl to withdraw Pemsel's 6.Gebirgs-Division from the Litsa.

Night, 8/9 October
Naval infantry attack German defences along the Srednyi Isthmus, and land from boats to attack them from the flank. The Barchenko and Leonov scout detachments also land and head towards Cape Krestovyi.

0800 hrs, 10 October
126th Light Rifle Corps, having marched 40km in 72 hours, captures the road junction west of Luostari. 127th Light Rifle Corps is following, and pushes on to the Tarnet Road.

10 October
131st Rifle Corps reaches the Russian Road with a regiment from 14th Rifle Division. 368th Rifle Division is sent to assist, but it arrives too late. A German counter-attack by retreating units of 6.Gebirgs-Division temporarily throws them off.

12 October
In the early morning, Barchenko and Leonov's scouts attack the batteries on Cape Krestovyi. The anti-aircraft battery is taken but the *Heeres-Küsten-Batterie* is not; however, it is neutralized by fire from higher terrain.

Late evening, 12 October
Timofeev's composite naval infantry battalion lands in Liinakhamari Bay. The *Heeres-Küsten-Batterie* on Cape Krestovyi is unable to fire at the landing boats.

12 October
6.Gebirgs-Division units have to cross the tundra to escape as Soviet units are on the Russian Road.

12–13 October
Shcherbakov sends 72nd Naval Rifle Brigade 15km north to the Tarnet Road, where 70th Naval Rifle Brigade is attempting to hold high ground south of the road. During the night, 72nd Naval Rifle Brigade reaches the road east of the Norwegian border.

1500 hrs, 13 October
Jodl realizes the escape route of 6.Gebirgs-Division is in danger. He communicates his concerns to Rendulic, and is given permission to attack the blocking position on the Tarnet Road.

Evening, 13 October
The Tarnet Road is cleared by soldiers from 2.Gebirgs-Division who are being pushed against from the east.

14 October
Soviet estimates claim 15,000–18,000 German soldiers are retreating along the Tarnet Road.

14 October	Soviet tanks capture the Speer Bridge, and the Prinz Eugen Bridge is vulnerable. Two battalions of Gebirgsjäger-Regiment 143 and three battalions of Grenadier-Brigade 388 are cut off. That night, they have to fight their way out.
0500 hrs, 15 October	Petsamo is captured. 150,000 mines and shells are seized in warehouses. Estimated German losses are 6,000 men.
15–18 October	The Germans send 2.Gebirgs-Division south towards Ivalo and 6.Gebirgs-Division north to Kirkenes. Shcherbakov orders a pause because of exhaustion and supply problems and splits his forces to pursue in both directions: 131st Rifle Corps and 99th Rifle Corps to Kirkenes from the east and south, respectively, and 31st Rifle Corps to Nikel and Nautsi in the south. The 126th Light Rifle Corps will attempt to cut off the German retreat from Kirkenes, and 127th Light Rifle Corps that from Nikel. The Northern Fleet will attempt to interdict German sea movement and also land additional naval infantry units.
20 October	367th Rifle Division is held up in front of Hill 441.4 on the Nikel Road; the Germans evacuate at night.
Morning, 22 October	Elements of 367th Rifle Division enter Nikel and capture the town by 1000 hrs. The 83rd Rifle Division is to launch the pursuit. On this day, one regiment with supporting armour is on the road beyond Nikel.
Night, 22/23 October	10th Guards Rifle Division uses a pontoon bridge at Holmfoss to outflank Gebirgsjäger-Regiment 143 further north and move on Kirkenes from the south.
24 October	14th Rifle Division advances to Bekfjord at Elvenes.
25 October	Kirkenes is captured by elements of 10th Guards Rifle Division. 14th Rifle Division crosses Bekfjord in assault boats.
25 October	A German position blocks 368th Rifle Division at Kaskama. The attempt to outflank the position fails. The retreat to Nautsi is resumed.
27 October	Nieden is captured, but the Germans have succeeded in withdrawing along Highway 50. The Soviets do not advance further along the road.
5 November	The Soviets, having captured Nautsi, enter Ivalo near Lake Inari. The Germans have already moved north-west into Norway.

OPPOSING COMMANDERS

SOVIET

Kirill Afanasyevich Meretskov was born in 1897 in Ryazan Province, and began his working life as a mechanic in Moscow. He was exempted from military service because of his profession, but was a committed revolutionary. He joined the Red Army in 1918 and was a commissar, being wounded three times. He went to the Frunze Military Academy and was appointed chief of staff of a cavalry division. In the 1920s and 1930s, he served in numerous appointments on the staff in the Moscow Military District, and then was made commander of the Leningrad Military District in January 1940, where he commanded 7th Army on operations. From August 1940 to January 1941, he was Chief of the General staff, but in June 1941, when he was sent to Leningrad as the representative of the High Command, he was arrested and interrogated. In September 1941, Stalin released him, and by December, he was commander of the Volkhov Front. He broke the encirclement of Leningrad in January 1943, and was transferred to command the Karelian Front in February 1944 when the Volkhov Front was disbanded. He launched the Svir–Petrozavodsk operation in June 1944, and following the Petsamo and Kirkenes operation in October, was made a Marshal of the Soviet Union. He was sent to command the Manchurian offensive in August 1945. Meretskov commanded military districts after the war, and was appointed Assistant Minister of Defence in 1955. He died in 1968.

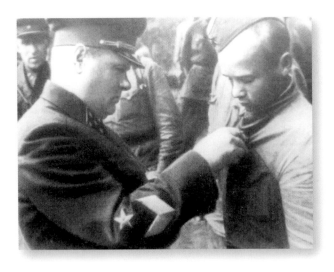

Meretskov (left) served in the north throughout the war, and was a leader that Stalin could not do without. (Public domain)

Arseny Grigorievich Golovko was born in 1906 in the Caucasus. He attended an agricultural college in Moscow, where he was drafted into the navy. He graduated from the Frunze Naval Academy in 1928 and specialized in torpedo boats, commanding a brigade in 1935. After graduating from the Naval Academy, he was chief of staff of the Northern Fleet, commander of the Caspian Flotilla and from 1940 to 1946 commander of the Northern Fleet. In 1950, he was appointed Chief of the Naval General Staff, and in 1956 commander of the Baltic Fleet. He died in 1962 through sickness probably

Rear Admiral Golovko became the commander of the Northern Fleet in 1940, and continued to serve in this role during the 1944 Petsamo and Kirkenes operation. (Sovfoto/UIG via Getty Images)

caused by his supervision of the nuclear tests at Novaya Zemlya in northern Russia.

Zinovy Nesterovich Alekseev was born in Kharkov in 1899. He served in the Red Army during the Civil War. He attended military school in Kiev in 1926 and then the Frunze Military Academy, graduating in 1934. By the end of 1938, he was chief of staff of a division in the Leningrad Military District. From August to October 1941, Alekseev commanded a People's Militia Division, during which time he was wounded. By December, he was back in staff appointments and by May 1943, commanded a division defending the line near Lake Onega. His division participated in the Svir–Petrozavodsk operation, and then he moved to command the 127th (in July) and 131st Rifle corps (in September). He served as a divisional commander after the war, and retired in 1953.

Colonel Vladimir Solovyov was born in 1902 in the Kursk region. In 1918, he was drafted into the Red Army, and was a platoon then company commander in the Ukraine. By 1935, he was a company commander in the 1st Rifle Regiment in Moscow. In 1939, Solovyov studied at the Frunze Military Academy. He worked on the army-level staff in the Leningrad Military District. In 1941, he graduated from the Higher Special (Intelligence) School of the General Staff. In June 1942, he commanded the 35th Guards Rifle Regiment and then in August the 6th Ski and Rifle Brigade (reorganized into the 31st Light Mountain Brigade in September). In February 1944, Solovyov was appointed commander of 1st Light Rifle Corps (renamed 126th Light Rifle Corps in March) and following the Petsamo and Kirkenes operation, deployed with his unit to Central Europe in March 1945. In 1950, he was assistant commander of 7th Mechanized Army. Solovyov retired from active duty in 1953.

Ivan Pavlovich Barchenko-Emelianov was born in Novgorod Province in 1915. He worked in a timber company, and then joined the naval infantry in 1939. He attended officer's school in Murmansk in 1941. He commanded a scout platoon, and then a scout company, and was assistant chief of staff of a battalion of 12th Naval Infantry Brigade in 1942. In 1943, Barchenko-Emelianov was appointed commander of the reconnaissance detachment of the Northern Defensive Region, and carried out numerous landings behind enemy lines. In the Petsamo operation, he commanded a detachment that was responsible for capturing the batteries on Cape Krestovyi, in order to ensure the success of the landings at Liinakhamari. He was then transferred to the Dniepr River naval flotilla. Barchenko-Emelianov served in the Baltic Fleet after the war, and then taught cadets at several naval schools. He was made a Hero of the Soviet Union after the Krestovyi raid.

Viktor Nikolaevich Leonov was born in Ryazan Province in 1916. He worked in a factory until joining the navy in 1937. Leonov served on submarines and then volunteered to serve in the 181st Separate Reconnaissance Detachment, carrying out raids behind enemy lines. In December 1942, he was commissar of the unit and in December 1943, he became its commander. He was promoted senior lieutenant in April 1944. In October 1944, he was tasked with capturing the 8.8cm gun battery on Cape Krestovyi. He was made a Hero of the Soviet Union after the Krestovyi operation. Leonov was deployed to Manchuria in early 1945, and led the 140th Separate Reconnaissance Detachment in the capture of Wonsan in Korea, when he again gained the award Hero of the Soviet Union. In 1950, he graduated from the Higher Naval School and in 1952, he was awarded the rank of Captain 2nd Rank. He also studied at the Naval Academy. Leonov died in 2003.

GERMAN

Generaloberst Lothar Rendulic was born in Austria in 1887. He was commissioned into the Austro–Hungarian Army in 1910. He fought in World War I on the Russian and Italian fronts. In 1932, Rendulic joined the Austrian National Socialist Party. He was suspended from the army, but returned after the annexation of Austria in 1938, and was commanding a division in 1940. In 1943, he commanded XXXV.Armee-Korps during the Battle of Kursk. Rendulic then moved to Yugoslavia, where he led 2.Panzer-Armee. In June 1944, Rendulic was sent to Lapland to lead 20.Gebirgs-Armee after Generaloberst Eduard Dietl was killed in a plane crash. In January 1945, he briefly commanded Heeresgruppe Kurland, and then moved to Heeresgruppe Nord from January to March, and Heeresgruppe Süd (which would be renamed Heeresgruppe Ostmark) in April and May. Rendulic was awarded the Swords to his Knight's Cross with Oak Leaves in January 1945 in recognition of his leadership in Lapland. He surrendered to US troops in May 1945 and was put on trial for war crimes, accused of ordering the execution of Yugoslavian civilians and the destruction of Rovaniemi in October 1944. Rendulic was cleared of the latter charge, but was sentenced to 20 years for the former. The sentence was reduced to 10 years, and he was released in 1951. He became involved in local politics in Austria, and died in 1971.

General der Gebirgstruppe **Ferdinand Jodl** was born in 1896. He served in a Bavarian artillery regiment during World War I, and then in the army of the Weimar Republic. By the start of World War II, he was an Oberstleutnant serving on an operational staff. In January 1942, Jodl was the chief of staff of what was to be named 20.Gebirgs-Armee, and in February was promoted to Generalmajor, and then to Generalleutnant a year later. He was made commander of XIX.Gebirgs-Korps in April 1944. In September that year, Jodl was promoted again, to General der Gebirgstruppe. He was awarded the Knight's Cross in January 1945, and surrendered in May that year in Norway. Jodl was not charged, and was released from captivity in 1947. He died in 1956.

Generalleutnant Hans Degen was born in 1899 in Bavaria. He was the nephew of Generaloberst Alfred Jodl, the Chief of the General Staff of the Oberkommando der Wehrmacht (OKW). Degen served in World War I. By 1938, he was the operations officer of 2.Gebirgs-Division. In July 1942, as Oberst, he was appointed the chief of staff of Gebirgskorps Norwegen, and in November 1943, the commander of 2.Gebirgs-Division. He remained in this position until February 1945. He was promoted to Generalmajor in January 1944, and Generalleutnant in September 1944. Severely wounded in February 1945, he was detained by US troops in May while in a military hospital. Degen was released from captivity in 1947.

Barchenko-Emelianov was the commander of the scout detachment that included both his Northern Defensive Region scout unit and Leonov's Northern Fleet scout detachment. Leonov was the commissar of the Northern Fleet scouts prior to being made its commander. Makar Babikov described how in the detachment, 'we for a long time had preferred to depend only on ourselves, on our own strength, not to count on casual attachments, not to place too much trust in those we did not know, with whom we had not trained. On more than one occasion, misfortune had followed if the detachment were joined up with someone' (quoted in M. Babikov, *Voyna v Arktika*, Moscow: Sovetskaya Rossiya, 1991, pp. 276–93). (Public domain)

OPPOSING FORCES

SOVIET

In addition to the two rifle divisions already in the northern Arctic in early 1944, the Soviets deployed another six in August that were organized into Group Pigarevich (45th Rifle Division, 3rd Naval Infantry Brigade and 2nd Fortified Region), and the 31st, 131st and 99th Rifle corps. Seven mortar regiments, 17 artillery regiments, three multiple rocket launcher regiments and two multiple rocket launcher brigades were brought in from the Karelian Front. In addition to these guns and mortars, each rifle regiment had 12 to 18 82mm mortars, four to six 120mm mortars and three to six 76mm guns; each rifle division also had on average a mix of 30 76mm and 122mm guns within its artillery regiment.

Many units were below establishment. The 99th Rifle Corps had 65 per cent of its authorized strength (19,157 men) because its 65th Rifle Division (6,641 men) had served on the Volkhov Front, and the other two rifle divisions – the 114th (6,418 men) and 368th (6,098 men) – had participated in the Svir–Petrozavodsk Operation in Karelia in June. The 65th Rifle Division was typical of the Soviet rifle divisions deployed in theatre, with three rifle regiments, each containing about 1,500 men. Each regiment had about 50 light machine guns, 24 heavy machine guns, 590 submachine guns, 620 rifles, 12 82mm mortars, four 120mm mortars, six 45mm guns and three 76mm guns. Some 45 mm anti-tank gun companies in the infantry regiments of other divisions were up to strength with three batteries each with four guns, though this was the exception. The artillery regiment of the division was equipped with 18 76mm and ten 122mm guns. In support, 99th Rifle Corps had 1,236th Artillery Regiment with 12 122mm and 12 152mm guns, and 471st Artillery Regiment with 16 150mm guns. The 99th Rifle Corps was also given the 989th Artillery Regiment, with 24 122mm guns; the 275th, 535th and 620th Mortar regiments,

Some of the naval infantry of the Soviet Light Rifle Corps were trained to march across tundra in any weather. In October, the terrain was on most days not covered with snow, and skis would not be necessary. (Sovfoto/UIG via Getty Images)

with 36 120mm mortars each; the 173rd Mortar Regiment, with 36 107mm mortars; and the 905th Mountain Artillery Regiment, with 24 76mm guns. This meant that on the day the offensive started, the two divisions in the first echelon of 99th Rifle Corps had 95 guns and mortars per kilometre of front. One or two artillery battalions and one or two mortar battalions would

The main artillery gun that served in the Soviet divisions was the 76mm M1939. Production of this weapon ceased at the end of 1941. (Sovfoto/UIG via Getty Images)

support each infantry battalion on the day of the attack. Each company on the main axis could expect the support of two to three artillery or mortar batteries. Whilst some divisional guns were set aside to support the 45mm guns in the direct fire role, the other supporting artillery units would be used in the indirect fire mode targeting enemy artillery, reserves and command and control.

The 131st Rifle Corps was the most experienced formation, with 10th Guards Rifle and 14th Rifle divisions having spent the entire war on the Murmansk Front. By comparison, 31st Rifle Corps's 83rd and 367th Rifle divisions (which were sent from the Karelian Front) had limited combat experience. Unit complements were similar to the 99th Rifle Corps. By the time of the second phase of the operation on 18 October, the main reinforcing units comprised 51st Cannon Artillery Regiment, with 18 152mm guns; 633rd Artillery Regiment, with 14 152mm guns; 989th Howitzer Artillery Regiment, with 24 122mm guns; 535th Mortar Regiment, with 36 120mm mortars; 482nd Mortar Regiment, with 34 120mm mortars; 44th and 64th Guards Mortar regiments, each with 24 multiple rocket launcher systems; and 1st Motorized Combat Engineer Brigade. The 48 multiple rocket launchers were to be used on the two strongest enemy defensive positions.

Naval infantry brigades were available for amphibious landings and deployed along the Srednyi Peninsula. Units of the Northern Defensive Region occupying defensive positions here included 12th Naval Infantry Brigade, and 347th and 348th Separate Naval Machine-Gun battalions. In reserve, Major-

The divisional gun that most divisions used was the 76mm M1942 ZiS-3, which had a lighter gun carriage than the M1939. Range was about 13.3km for both guns. (Sovfoto/UIG via Getty Images)

General E. T. Dubovtsev also had 349th Separate Naval Machine-Gun Battalion and one tank company; for amphibious operations, he had the 63rd Naval Infantry Brigade with the attached 716th Chemical Platoon, one sapper company of the 388th Separate Engineer Battalion, a platoon of the dock-amphibious company and the reconnaissance detachments of Northern Defensive Region and Headquarters, Northern Fleet.

Naval infantry brigades were organized into two light rifle corps in order to carry out wide outflanking moves around the German right flank. Both light rifle corps

The difficulty bringing guns forward made mortars more important to sustaining a rapid advance. The mortar had a range of 5,700m. The crew of this 120mm PM-43 mortar are resting. (TASS via Getty Images)

Soviet commanders were keen to deploy the heavy KV-85 tanks armed with an 85mm gun to the northern Arctic, and so they were brought across Kola Inlet. The 73rd Separate Guards Heavy Tank Regiment was formed in May 1944, and had only limited combat experience. (Courtesy of the Central Museum of the Armed Forces, Moscow via Stavka)

were established in March 1944. The 126th Light Rifle Corps included the 31st Light Rifle Brigade and the 72nd Naval Rifle Brigade. The 127th Light Rifle Corps had the 69th and 70th Naval Rifle Brigades. The four brigades all had three battalions (each of 715 men), an artillery battalion equipped with 12 76mm guns, a mortar battalion with eight 120mm mortars and 16 82mm mortars, a submachine gun company, an Anti-Tank Rifle company, an anti-aircraft platoon, a signal company, an engineer company, a transportation company and a medical company. Authorized strength was 4,334 men, 178 vehicles and 818 horses. However, the brigades were not thought to have any vehicles or carts, and relied on mules and reindeer. Each light rifle corps was thought to also have an artillery battalion of 12 76mm mountain guns and a mortar battalion of 12 120mm mortars, and was equivalent to an infantry division. The 127th Light Rifle Corps, because of losses suffered in the summer offensive in southern Karelia, would be in the second echelon.

Armour

Soviet tank forces supported the offensive (110 tanks and self-propelled guns) but did not accompany the naval riflemen, as the absence of roads and suitable cross-country terrain limited their utility. The 7th Guards Tank Brigade, with 37 T-34s and commanded by Colonel N. Yurenkov; 89th Separate Tank Regiment, with 18 T-34s and commanded by Lieutenant-Colonel Ye. Suchkov; 339th Guards Heavy Self-Propelled Artillery Regiment, with 17 ISU-152s; 378th Guards Heavy Self-Propelled Artillery Regiment; and Lieutenant-Colonel N. Arshinevskiy's 73rd Separate Guards Heavy Tank Regiment, with 21 KV-85s were all transported across the bay by barge and driven to 8–12km from the German front line by 7 October. The 378th Guards Heavy Self-Propelled Artillery Regiment and 73rd Separate Guards Heavy Tank Regiment were attached to 131st Rifle Corps; they were sent to support 10th Guards Rifle Division. The 7th Guards Tank Brigade and 339th Guards Heavy Self-Propelled Artillery Regiment were attached to 99th Rifle Corps and would be used by the second echelon infantry, with 2nd Combat Engineer Battalion in support. The 89th Separate Tank Regiment did not arrive until after 7 October and was in the army reserve.

The 73rd Separate Guards Heavy Tank Regiment was formed in May 1944 on the Kola Peninsula. In September, the tanks were loaded onto railcars and made their way to Murmansk; there they were

ferried across the Kola Inlet and started a 75km road march to the front. Arshinevskiy (1985) described how the problems operating tanks in this terrain – the lack of roads, the steep rises and falls, peat moss, large boulders, streams and natural escarpments – slowed the rate of advance. He described how the advance on the Bolshoi Karikvayvish elevation needed his tanks to negotiate slopes of over 25 degrees. The tank's use of ammunition would be prolific. In 18 days of combat, 73rd Separate Guards Heavy Tank Regiment would use 4,270 main-gun rounds, 90,000 rifle rounds in the co-axial machine gun, 70,000 submachine guns rounds and 530 grenades.

Engineers

The difficulty of the terrain presented an extensive engineering problem. The road network needed improvement and the rocky terrain and strong defensive positions gave the engineers a combat role, too. The Soviets deployed 30 engineer battalions. Each division had an integral engineer battalion, and the 20th Svirsk Motorized Assault Combat Engineer Brigade supporting 99th Rifle Corps and 13th Assault Combat Engineer Brigade supporting 131st Rifle Corps had six battalions each. The 1st

The Soviets also sent heavy assault guns to the northern Arctic, including two regiments that had the ISU-152, seen here. Armed with a 152mm gun, the armoured vehicle was capable of knocking out German bunkers, providing it could target them. (From the fonds of the RGAKFD in Krasnogorsk via Stavka)

Motorized Engineer Brigade also deployed three battalions. In addition, there were two pontoon-bridge battalions, a road exploitation battalion, a road construction battalion and a battalion of demolition specialists. Also, the 275th and 284th Separate Special Purpose Motorized battalions, supporting 131st and 99th Rifle Corps respectively, were equipped with 94 amphibious vehicles.

Special purpose road-building groups were formed at divisional level, with a battalion of infantry often designated to support the engineer battalion. Entire rifle regiments could be assigned to road building if necessary. Engineers were also used in a reconnaissance capacity, to move into German rear areas prior to the start of the offensive to attack German infrastructure and search for routes to cross the Titovka River. Engineer units belonging to the divisions were responsible for finding out the extent of German defensive positions, locating suitable routes to build roads on and helping to reduce enemy strong points.

Assault groups within the infantry units in the first echelon were formed with an infantry platoon having an engineer section attached. The 20th Svirsk Motorized Assault Combat Engineer Brigade attached its 109th and 135th Combat Engineer battalions to 65th Rifle Division for the Titovka crossings to participate in assault groups; 222nd Combat Engineer Battalion was assigned to 114th Rifle Division for their assault groups; 447th Combat Engineer Battalion was given the task of building the bridge across the Titovka; 28th Flamethrower Battalion was assigned to the assault sections along the front; and 50th Separate Road Exploitation Battalion would build a road in the 65th Rifle Division's area. In addition, 218th Road Construction Battalion would build a road in 114th Rifle Division's

Soviet aircraft were deployed to the Arctic in large numbers, frequently (though not exclusively) having to operate from locations that had motorized support. (TASS via Getty Images)

area; and 168th Bridge Construction Battalion would build another bridge over the Titovka.

Aviation

Lieutenant-General I. M. Sokolov had at his disposal four mixed air divisions, a bomber division and two fighter divisions. A mixed air division was assigned to both 99th and 131st Rifle corps, and their commanders located their command posts alongside the army commanders. A liaison officer was attached to each infantry division to bring in close air support. Another liaison officer was attached to the tank forces of each rifle corps. Sokolov was in control of the bomber division, two mixed air divisions and the two fighter divisions and was located with Shcherbakov. Air superiority would be maintained by bombing German airfields at Luostari, Kirkenes and Salmijärvi, and the fighters would maintain patrols to ensure air superiority. Battlefield air interdiction would target enemy reserves and hinder movement to and from the front line. In total, the Karelian Front had 747 aircraft available.

Naval

In October 1944, the Northern Fleet was employing the following assets for operations in Varangerfjord: six to eight submarines, 20 torpedo cutters, 10 large submarine chasers, and eight to 12 small submarine chasers. The Northern Fleet had 275 aircraft, including 55 bombers, 35 ground attack planes, 160 fighters and some utility and transport planes. A total of 8,907 sorties would be flown, including 1,127 in support of naval ground forces; most were against German naval traffic. Northern Fleet aircraft would also target German ships in Kirkenes port, and whilst they were at sea if discovered by aerial reconnaissance.

The Soviets used fighters like the Yak-3 shown here to fly patrols to maintain air supremacy, but often German bombers did get through to launch attacks on advancing Soviet ground units. (TASS via Getty Images)

The importance of the navy in transporting army units and supplies across Kola Bay prior to the start of the offensive was crucial in ensuring units were in position on time. According to Admiral Arsenyi Golovko, the navy ferried 118 tanks and self-propelled guns, 237 guns, 143 tracked prime movers, 271 vehicles, 20,000 tons of cargo and 25,000 men.

GERMAN

The XIX.Gebirgs-Korps comprised 2.Gebirgs and 6.Gebirgs divisions, Division van der Hoop and 210.Infanterie-Division. The *Gebirgs-Divisionen* were smaller than *Infanterie-Divisionen* and had reduced transport units, but included

1,110 horse-drawn wagons, 4,000 mules and 1,500 horses, and 900 vehicles and 450 motorcycles. The greater number of mules and horses was particularly useful for transporting equipment because there were few roads. The 2.Gebirgs-Division had 16,026 men as of 1 September 1944, equipped with 13,873 rifles and submachine guns, 514 machine guns, 45 field guns and six 7.5cm anti-tank guns. The 6.Gebirgs-Division, including the attached Grenadier-Brigade 388, had 18,020 men with 12,621 rifles and submachine guns, 36 field guns and

nine 7.5cm anti-tank guns. Whilst the Gebirgsjäger had 81mm mortars available, there were no 120mm mortars. In total, as of 1 July 1944, XIX.Gebirgs-Korps had 245 mortars, 120 3.7cm anti-tank guns and 109 Panzerschreck anti-tank rocket launchers. Radfahr-Aufklärungs-Brigade Norwegen, formed in April 1944 with two battalions each with four companies, was available to XIX.Gebirgs-Korps.

Division van der Hoop (Grenadier-Brigade 193 and Grenadier-Brigade 503), commanded by Oberst Adrian Freiheer van der Hoop, as of 1 September 1944 had 3,992 soldiers but no field or anti-tank guns; the division held positions along the coast to the Titovka River, including Petsamo Bay and the Srednyi Peninsula. Grenadier-Brigade 503 was originally Luftwaffe Feld Regiment 503, which was formed on 1 December 1942 from disbanded Luftwaffe construction battalions. On 1 November 1943, the regiment was transferred to the Heer. Major Georg Gebhard was the III.Bataillon commander and had served with 6.Gebirgs-Division. Grenadier-Brigade 193 (as Infanterie-Regiment 193 with three battalions) had fought in the invasion of Norway in 1940; the unit stayed in the region, and in 1942 was renamed a Grenadier-Regiment. The regiment lost the second battalion in 1942. Grenadier-Brigade 388 (with three battalions) was also established that month from Infanterie-Regiment 388, which had participated in the invasion of Norway. The 210.Infanterie-Division had five battalions with 77 field guns in static defensive positions along the Norwegian coast at Tana, Vardø, Vadsø, Kirkenes and Tarnet.

There were also numerous coastal batteries. Marine-Küsten-Batterie 1/517 on Cape Romanov, commanded by Oberleutnant Sensenhauser, comprised four 15cm SK C/28 artillery pieces in twin mounts. Marine-Küsten-Batterie 2/517, comprising four 15cm L/40 guns and two 15cm SK C/28 guns in a twin turret, was located at the headland on the west side of Petsamofjord. Heeres-Küsten-Batterie 1/773 (at Cape Krestovyi, on the southern side of Liinakhamari Bay), with four 15.5cm K418(f) guns, and Heeres-Küsten-Batterie 2/773 (on the northern side of the bay), with two 21cm K39/40 guns, were located further down the fjord. The 3./gemischte Flak-Abteilung 302 was also on Cape Krestovyi.

In Lapland the German Army had access to captured artillery pieces that were formed into field artillery battalions, to be used by the army commander. Some German heavy gun battalions, notably the SS battalion that was deployed in the northern Arctic, were motorized, and benefited from the new roads that were built in the region. (Martin Sachse/Ullstein Bild via Getty Images)

The baggage trains of the Gebirgs-Division battalions deployed on the Titovka relied on horse-drawn transport. (Nik Cornish at www.Stavka.org.uk)

German positions built for infantry were often difficult to camouflage because of the absence of foliage in the northern Arctic. When the weather worsened, snow was more effective at hiding their presence from Soviet reconnaissance aircraft. (Martin Sachse/Ullstein Bild via Getty Images)

Some *Heeres-Küsten-Batterie* also formed field artillery units equipped with captured Polish 15.5cm howitzers and 10.5cm K331 guns.

Navy

Of the German ships located in northern Norwegian ports, the Soviets believed that the following were most likely to be employed against the ships of Northern Fleet: two to four destroyers; 20–25 patrol ships, minesweepers and cutters; and 10 fast amphibious barges. The Germans would use the ships to evacuate men and supplies from Kirkenes.

Aviation

German aviation assets in the Murmansk sector were based on airfields at Luostari, Høybuktmoen (Kirkenes), Nautsi, Salmijärvi and at other locations. By 1 October 1944, 109 aircraft were operating from these bases. Air reconnaissance was carried out primarily by fighter aircraft that reconnoitred the forward edge of the Soviet defences and the road system leading to it with 10–12 sorties per day. Dive-bombers would be used in close air support.

ORDERS OF BATTLE

SOVIET

14TH ARMY

Army Reserve
89th Separate Tank Brigade
1st Motorized Engineer Brigade
50th Separate Road Exploitation Battalion
218th Separate Road Construction Battalion
168th Bridge Construction Battalion
1st Separate Guards Engineer Battalion
96th Separate Motorized Pontoon Battalion
Group Pigarevich
45th Rifle Division
3rd Naval Infantry Brigade
2nd Fortified Region
31st Rifle Corps
83rd Rifle Division
367th Rifle Division
131st Rifle Corps
10th Guards Rifle Division
14th Rifle Division
Attached
73rd Separate Guards Heavy Tank Regiment
378th Guards Heavy Self-Propelled Artillery Regiment
13th Assault Combat Engineer Brigade
275th Separate Special Purpose Motorized Battalion
99th Rifle Corps
65th Rifle Division
114th Rifle Division
368th Rifle Division

Attached
7th Guards Tank Brigade
339th Guards Heavy Self-Propelled Artillery Regiment
20th Motorised Assault Combat Engineer
284th Separate Special Purpose Motorized Battalion
126th Light Rifle Corps
31st Light Rifle Brigade
72nd Naval Rifle Brigade
127th Light Rifle Corps
69th Naval Rifle Brigade
70th Naval Rifle Brigade

GERMAN

XIX.GEBIRGS-KORPS

Radfahr-Aufklärungs-Brigade Norwegen
2.Gebirgs-Division
Gebirgsjäger-Regiment 137
Gebirgsjäger-Regiment 136
Gebirgs-Artillerie-Regiment 111
6.Gebirgs-Division
Gebirgsjäger-Regiment 141
Gebirgsjäger-Regiment 143
Gebirgs-Artillerie-Regiment 118
Grenadier-Brigade 388
Division van der Hoop
Grenadier-Brigade 503
Grenadier-Brigade 193
210.Infanterie-Division

OPPOSING PLANS

SOVIET

The need to seize the road net would dominate the battle. The offensive on the left flank would take priority because of the Lanweg's close proximity to the front line. The 99th and 131st Rifle corps, followed by 31st Rifle Corps in reserve, would attack the German right flank whilst Group Pigarevich would keep 6.Gebirgs-Division occupied on the Litsa River. The 126th and 127th Light Rifle corps would carry out a deep envelopment by moving around Hill 237.1, and capture the road junction west of Luostari. On the Soviet right, once the army's attack had gathered momentum, 12th Naval Infantry Brigade would attack across the Srednyi Isthmus, and 63rd Naval Infantry Brigade would land on the coastline. As well as interdicting the Germans at sea, the Northern fleet was ordered to establish a naval base, and in order to accomplish this Golovko's staff planned an amphibious landing to seize Liinakhamari on the west shore of Petsamofjord.

In the summer, a 15km strip had separated the two sides. The 10th Guards Rifle Division seized this area in order to build a road that would join with the Lanweg. Each kilometre took a week, and the work was carried out mostly at night. On 2 September, the 35th Guards Rifle Regiment received the order to advance to the enemy line near Lake Chapr. This was done successfully, and counter-attacks were repelled. The division occupied positions south of the lake in front of the Bolshoi Karikvayvish elevation.

On 29 September, Meretskov visited divisional headquarters to explain the plan. The breakthrough site chosen was the 9km between the lake and height 237.1. The objective was to seize Luostari, before advancing north and then liberating Petsamo. The 10th Guards Rifle and 14th Rifle divisions of 131st Rifle Corps would be in the first echelon. Initially, the Lanweg was given to 65th Rifle Division to use, but Meretskov was persuaded that 10th Guards Rifle Division could have use of it if they got to the Titovka River first.

On the Srednyi Isthmus, up to 700 linear metres of barbed-wire obstacles were destroyed, 846 Soviet mines were removed and five pressure-activated high-explosive devices were neutralized in 37 penetrations of the barrier system in the week prior to the main attack. Infantry and artillery units of the Northern Defensive Region carefully compiled information about the German dispositions with the help of reconnaissance patrols, prisoner interrogations and daily observation. (Nik Cornish at www.Stavka.org.uk)

The Srednyi Peninsula

Golovko planned the breakthrough of enemy defences on the isthmus of Srednyi Peninsula, and the capture of the Titovka–Porovaara road to cut the enemy's path of retreat to Petsamo. One brigade, with the support and cover of surface ships and aviation, would reach Hill 388.9 to interdict the Titovka–Porovaara road. The other was to land on the southern coast of Maattivuono Bay into the rear of the defences. The amphibious landing was to occur immediately prior to the breakthrough attack on the Srednyi Peninsula. The joint force was ordered to reach the southern shore of Lake Seljärvi within the first day, within two days Rosvatunturi and Lake Ustojärvi, and within three days the Titovka–Porovaara road and occupy positions from Larasjärvi to Hill 388.9.

The assault was to be supported by the preliminary suppression of batteries on the coastline of Petsamovuono Bay and on the isthmus by Northern Defensive Region artillery and Northern Fleet air forces three days prior to the attack. A 30-minute artillery barrage by Northern Defensive Region guns on enemy command posts, firing positions and soldiers just prior to the breakthrough would also take place. Two destroyers were to be positioned in Motovskiy Bay to support the breakthrough on the isthmus of Srednyi Peninsula. Up to 275 aircraft of the Northern Fleet were to protect the fleet against enemy air attacks, conduct air reconnaissance and attack enemy forces at sea and on land. This number included an operational group, consisting of 10 Il-2 Shturmoviks, 10 Yaks and 10 Kittyhawks, based on Pummanki Airfield. To distract the enemy's attention, the operational plan provided for a demonstration landing on the coastline of Motovskiy Bay between Cape Pikshuev and Cape Mogilnyi.

On 9 October, Admiral Golovko with his mobile staff were positioned on Hill 342.0, with Major General Yefim Dubovtsev, commander of Northern Fleet naval infantry forces, and the 12th Naval Infantry Brigade commander nearby. Commander of the Torpedo Cutter Brigade, Captain 1st Rank Kuzmin, deployed to Hill 200 near Pummanki, as did the commander of Fleet Air Forces Major-General Preobrazhenskyi. The positioning of command posts close to each other and the area of operations permitted these senior commanders to have observation of the offensive, and helped rapid and reliable communications, the receiving of timely and precise information on the situation and coordination between them.

Cutter crews practised rapid approaches to shorelines, placement of special gangplanks on the shore and landing of the assault force and unloading of weapons. Special attention was given to holding the bow of the cutter to the shore during the ebb and flow of the surf by manipulating the throttles, firing from cutters, laying down smoke screens and manoeuvering in smoke during the approach to or withdrawal from shore, and the removal of the cutter from rocks. Torpedoes were removed from torpedo cutters, and depth-charge launchers, acoustical ranging equipment and other extraneous equipment was removed from the small and large sub chasers. Additional radio communications gear was placed onboard cutters designated for the amphibious force commander and the landing force commanders. Pathfinders were tasked with the identification and marking of landing sites on the shore before the approach of the main landing force. SP-95 marking lights, as the most transportable, would be utilized. Three pairs of alignment lights and two navigational lights were established on the land to assist the ships in crossing from Pummanki to Maattivuono Bay. Altogether, naval infantry

participated in one brigade-level, 16 battalion-level and 28 company-level tactical exercises for the purpose of training the units in their actions ashore after the landing.

The 12th Naval Infantry Brigade practised close combat, the rapid assembly of subunits in mountainous terrain, and land navigation and terrain orientation at night. Each squad was equipped with assault ladders and ropes for surmounting steep slopes and descents. Each battalion assembled two or three assault groups for blocking and destroying enemy firing positions during the breakthrough; each of these groups rehearsed on specially prepared terrain similar in nature to the terrain the actual combat would occur on. In total, 14 company-level, 10 battalion-level, and two brigade-level exercises were conducted, principally at night. Officers focused on the occupation of start positions prior to the attack, coordination between and within units and the maintenance of continuous command and control during battle. Artillery officers held joint field exercises with infantry officers to establish terrain orientation points and mutual signals. Infantry officers showed the artillery where to blow lanes in the barbed-wire obstacles, the enemy firing positions to suppress and in what order to shift fires from one line to another. Forward observer teams enabled infantry commanders to communicate with artillery units; six were sent to the battalion in the first echelon, and had common numerical designators for targets, order of priority for forward observers and call signs and frequencies for maintaining communication. Reconnaissance had determined the location of six artillery and 15 mortar batteries and engineer fortifications.

The Northern Fleet Air Force and the Soviet Air Force would provide close air support to soldiers fighting in close proximity to the Germans, especially on Cape Krestovyi. This required measures to be in place to ensure the correct targets were being attacked. Here, Soviet pilots plan their route. (Courtesy of the Central Museum of the Armed Forces, Moscow via Stavka)

From 6 to 10 October, on the Srednyi Peninsula six reconnaissance parties totalling 236 personnel prepared 37 lanes in the barbed-wire obstacles, varying in width from 4m to 70m, and removed 846 Soviet mines from five Soviet minefields in the attack sector. At 0320 hrs on the morning of 10 October, engineer troops and attached naval infantry groups detonated demolitions and line charges in the enemy barbed-wire obstacles, resulting in the creation of a 1km-long passage lane.

Logistics

The maintenance of logistical support to the front needed forward planning to be successful. In September, ammunition was stockpiled and units had a six-day supply of food and forage. The army supply depots stocked a seven-day supply of food and 14 of forage. Ten days' supply of food was in Murmansk. Supplies had to be brought forward by road or barge. Some 800 metric tons of supplies were needed every day to keep the army fed and able to fight. Around 64,500m^3 of firewood was available to be used for heating. The Karelian Front had seven truck battalions that were capable of moving over 1,700 metric tons in a single lift. With the absence of roads, horses and mules provided critical support in moving supplies. A horse was able to carry over 250lb, a reindeer 75–80lb. Each division had nearly 1,000 horses in its complement.

The Titovka River plan

The 10th Guards Rifle Division faced the Malyy (Small) Karikvayvish (Katschberg position) elevation that had numerous folds. In the north, the slopes were flat and gently sloped down to Lake Chapr; to the south they broke off steeply and only gradually began to fall in the distance. The division on the eastern slopes could not see the reverse slope. In order to hit the German guns with counter-battery fire, a group of forward observers commanded by Guard Senior Lieutenant N. Galchenko with two radio operators was sent out at night to observe enemy rear-area positions and report on the movement of their reserves. The scouts helped with the identification of enemy positions and fortifications, too. The importance of terrain and the strength of the German positions were better evaluated because of their work.

The 28th Guards Rifle Regiment would attack from the north with the 24th Guards Rifle Regiment from the south. The 35th Guards Rifle Regiment would follow the 28th Guards Rifle Regiment, as German defences were stronger here. The first echelon would not only capture defensive fortifications with their first battalions, they would also clear them and use their second battalions to maintain the momentum of the offensive once the height was captured. The regiments would not have a reserve, but a powerful enemy counter-attack was not expected and this risk was thought to be worth taking. This plan was used because the Soviets thought the Germans would wait until the first echelon had passed and then fight the second echelon regiment that was usually used to exploit. To the south, 65th Rifle Division would attack the Bolshoi (Large) Karikvayvish (Venediger position), a higher elevation that could see into the 10th Guards Rifle Division area. The 24th Rifle Regiment was formed into three echelons to guard against the eventuality that this position might not be taken quickly.

The Soviet planners made sure they had a 3:1 superiority on the main axis of advance. In fact their assessment of the strength of 2.Gebirgs-Division was incorrect; the force ratio was about 4.3:1. Some 1,600 Soviet guns and mortars were opposed here by what the Soviets thought were 431 guns and mortars. On 2 October, after discussing the plan with Shcherbakov, Major-General Mikulskii, the commander of 99th Rifle Corps, went over the terrain with his three divisional commanders. The next day, the divisional commanders walked the terrain with their regimental commanders. By 4 October, the battalion commanders were taking their company commanders on a reconnaissance. On 7 October, at 0800 hrs, the bombardment would commence.

GERMAN

The German defensive line was not continuous, but based on a series of company- or platoon-strength fortifications on dominating heights that had bunkers, connecting trenches, fire positions and supply caches. Gebirgsjäger-Regiment 137 occupied these positions and had available Gebirgs-Artillerie-Regiment 111; a battalion from the regiment was designated to support each of the battalions of Gebirgsjäger-Regiment 137, and the fourth was kept in reserve to be allocated as required. The positions were between two and four kilometres from each other, and intervening low ground was covered with mines and patrolled regularly. Other defensive belts further back along the Titovka River (10–12km from the first) and Petsamo River (20–25km from the second) that covered road or pathway approaches to the rivers were not yet occupied. The mines at Nikel and the ports of Liinakhamari and Kirkenes also had defensive positions prepared.

The German defences forward of the Titovka, commanded by Major Grumm of Gebirgsjäger-Regiment 137, were divided into three zones: Zacharias, occupied by Hauptmann Neuburg's I./Gebirgsjäger-Regiment 137 in *Stützpunkte* (Strongpoints) Wallberg, Zuckerhutl and Rabenkopf; Viktor, occupied by Hauptmann G. von Strachwitz's II./Gebirgsjäger-Regiment 137 in Ortler and Venediger; and Karl, occupied by Hauptmann Junker with III./Gebirgsjäger-Regiment 137 in Katschberg and numerous platoon positions. Zacharias was to be supported by II./Gebirgs-Artillerie-Regiment 111; Viktor by III./Gebirgs-Artillerie-Regiment 111; and Karl by I./Gebirgs-Artillerie-Regiment 111. The IV.(s)/SS-Gebirgs-Artillerie-Regiment 6 was designated the Schwerpunktgruppe with one 14.5cm *Zug*, one 10.5cm *Zug* and one 7.5cm *Pak Zug*.

Hauptmann Neuburg in Wallberg had one *Zug* from 1./Gebirgsjäger-Regiment 137 with four light machine guns, three 5cm mortars and two 8cm mortars with 800 rounds. In Zuckerhutl there was the rest of 1./Gebirgsjäger-Regiment 137, one *Zug* from 4./Gebirgsjäger-Regiment 137, an *Infanterie-Geschütz Zug*, a *Pionier Zug*, and two *Gruppen* from 1./Pionier-Bataillon 82 with 13 light machine guns and four heavy machine guns with 145,000 rounds, two 8cm mortars with 2,100 rounds, two light infantry guns with 1,600 rounds and two 3.7cm anti-tank guns

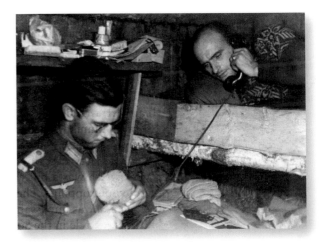

German positions on the Srednyi Isthmus in particular, and forward of the Titovka, were built and maintained for three years and were comfortable for the garrison. Those on the Titovka were not even exposed to artillery fire, as the main Soviet line was initially miles away. (Hanns Hubmann/Ullstein Bild via Getty Images)

German positions were hardened and offered good protection from the effects of artillery bombardment. On a single kilometre of front from Mustatunturi ridge to Hill 109.0 (south of Kutovaya), the Soviets assessed the Germans as having: 800m of communications trenches; 4.3km of barbed-wire obstacles; 10 mortars; six guns; seven heavy machine guns; 20 light machine guns; 43 MP 40 automatic rifles; 420 rifles; and 520 infantry soldiers. The most vulnerable defence was along the coastline of Maattivuono Bay. Ammunition supplies were hoarded and initially plentiful. (Nik Cornish at www. Stavka.org.uk)

with 770 rounds. In Rabenkopf there were 3./Gebirgsjäger-Regiment 137, the *Pionier Zug* of III./Gebirgsjäger-Regiment 137, one *Gruppe* from 1./Pionier-Bataillon 82, and the *Pionier Zug* from Radfahr-Aufklärungs-Brigade Norwegen with 12 light machine guns (46,000 rounds) and one 8cm mortar (75 rounds). Hauptmann Neuberg was based in Rainerlager.

Hauptmann Strachwitz in Ortler had 2./Feld-Ersatz-Bataillon 111, one *Zug* of 9./Gebirgsjäger-Regiment 137, one *Zug* of 1./Pionier-Bataillon 82, and the headquarters of 5./Gebirgs-Artillerie-Regiment 111 with four heavy machine guns, eight light machine guns (195,000 rounds), one 3.7cm Pak gun (408 rounds) and four 8cm mortars (2,550 rounds). Venediger position had 6./Gebirgsjäger-Regiment 137, one *Gruppe* from 9./Gebirgsjäger-Regiment 137, the *Pionier Zug* of II./Gebirgsjäger-Regiment 137, one *Zug* from 1./Pionier-Bataillon 82, one heavy machine gun and one 8cm mortar *Gruppe* from 1./82 Pionier-Bataillon, the *Pionier Zug* from III./Gebirgsjäger-Regiment 136, the *Infanterie-Geschütz Zug* from II./Gebirgsjäger-Regiment 137, and one *Zug* from Radfahr-Aufklärungs-Brigade Norwegen with 12 light machine guns and six heavy machine guns (335,160 rounds), five 81mm mortars (3,250 rounds), two light infantry guns (1,780 rounds) and two 3.7cm Pak guns (816 rounds). Strachwitz was in Isarlager on the Titovka River. *Riegelstellungen* (bolt positions) Vevi and Veronika were garrisoned by 4./Feld-Ersatz-Bataillon 111.

Hauptmann Junker in Katschberg had 7./Gebirgsjäger-Regiment 137 less one *Zug*, one heavy machine-gun *Gruppe* from 9./Gebirgsjäger-Regiment 137, one *Zug* from Radfahr-Aufklärungs-Brigade Norwegen, two *Züge* from 3./Pionier-Bataillon 82, and one Infanterie-Geschütz gun from 10./Gebirgsjäger-Regiment 137 with ten light machine guns and two heavy machine guns (174,600 rounds), three 8cm mortars (1,900 rounds), one light infantry gun (896 rounds) and one 3.7cm Pak gun (408 rounds). Platoon position Kathrein had one *Zug* from 7./Gebirgsjäger-Regiment 137; Araberberg had an 8cm mortar and two *Züge* from 8./Gebirgsjäger-Regiment 137; Tartarenkopf Süd (Toni) had one *Zug* from 8./Gebirgsjäger-Regiment 137, one *Gruppe* from 9./Gebirgsjäger-Regiment 137, the *Pionier Zug* of II./Gebirgsjäger-Regiment 136, and two *Gruppen* from the Pionier unit belonging to Radfahr-Aufklärungs-Brigade Norwegen; Trichterhöhe had 13./Gebirgsjäger-Regiment 137; and Tartarenkopf Nord (Trudel) had 12./Gebirgsjäger-Regiment 137.

The two battalions of Gebirgsjäger-Regiment 136 that were present (II and III) were in reserve along the Lanweg. The II./Gebirgsjäger-Regiment 136 was commanded by Hauptmann Ruepp and III./Gebirgsjäger-Regiment 136 by Hauptmann Förschl.

The Soviets described the Venediger position in detail. The Bolshoi Karikvayvish was a hill with steep rocky slopes, and in places, unclimbable granite outcroppings. The terrain near the approaches to the hill, covered in rock debris, was impassable even for tracked vehicles. The position presented like a semi-circle in the Soviet positions and flanked the approaches to other

German defensive positions from the south and north-east. A circular trench system went around the top of the hill, and communication trenches linked the command posts, dugouts and most important firing positions. The trenches were mostly carved into the rock and partially brick-lined. Firing points were either dug into the rocks or overlaid with stone on a cement base. To the rear aspect of the trenches were concrete sleeping bunkers dug into the rock.

Foxholes were dug into the trenches, and nearby were firing platforms for machine guns, light guns and mortars. Short branch trenches were dug to these positions from the main trench line. Ammunition dumps were distributed in light shelters near the trenches. Repair facilities, the aid station, food supply dumps, equipment and engineer items were located on the reverse slopes of the hill. The strongpoints were belted by two lines of barbed-wire obstacles to a height of 3m and spiral in form, and there was an anti-personnel minefield in five to six rows. The defensive complex had telephone communications that facilitated tactical coordination with the neighbouring strongpoints and resistance nodes on other heights.

At the isthmus on the Srednyi Peninsula, in front of Northern Defensive Region, the Germans occupied a defensive line they had established in August 1941 that stretched from the southern shore of Maattivuono Bay along Mustatunturi Range to heights 122.0 and 109.0, and then to Kutovaya Inlet. The German defensive line was a system of contiguous company defensive positions composed of platoon strongpoints that consisted of two or three permanent and 10–12 temporary or open firing positions, interconnected with trenches and joined with a command post and dugouts in the rear. Between the firing positions, the trenches had embrasures to accommodate rifles and machine guns. The Germans had as many as 200 permanent and up to 800 temporary or open-type firing positions on the isthmus. The defensive line was up to three kilometres deep. In the majority of cases, dugouts were constructed deep in the rock faces and were well protected against artillery fire. Many bomb shelters and tunnels had been dug into the rocks. The III./Grenadier-Brigade 193, II./Grenadier-Brigade 503 and III./Grenadier-Brigade 503 occupied these positions.

Blocking the approaches to the strongpoints were two or three rows of barbed wire, mines and explosive demolitions. The barbed wire was set up like a fence on wooden posts or stakes, as rolls of concertina wire, or simply scattered about. Fastened to the barbed wire were special cartridges and signal rockets that flared upwards when the wire was touched, signalling danger. Deep in the German defensive line were separate centres of resistance and barrier systems covered by fire.

The heavily broken terrain consisted of bare, rocky mountains, with many lakes, streams and creeks between them that greatly hindered the movement of infantry. The movement of artillery, tanks and carts was possible only along specific roads. In some areas, such as Lake Suormusjärvi to Porovaara, the Mustatunturi Range had only a single improved dirt road, 4m wide at the most, with areas to permit the passing of approaching traffic.

The two Gebirgs-Artillerie regiments that supported the Gebirgs-Division had some le FH 18/40 10.5cm guns that were lighter than the gun used by infantry divisions. This 10.5cm gun belongs to a Gebirgs-Artillerie-Regiment. (Nik Cornish at www. Stavka.org.uk)

THE CAMPAIGN

THE FIRST PHASE, 7–13 OCTOBER 1944

Crossing the Titovka

At 0800 hrs on 7 October, the Soviets began their artillery bombardment. Some 100,000 rounds were fired in 2h 35m. In low areas, a fog carried in from the north brought low clouds; the hilltops were also occasionally shrouded in mist. At 0900 hrs, heavy snow started to fall. The artillery started to slow their firing from 0935 hrs because observing and correcting fire was hampered by poor visibility. When, at 1035 hrs, fire was shifted to targets further back, the first echelon infantry units attacked. Their objective was to seize crossings over the Titovka by the end of the day, 9–10km from their start position.

In the 10th Guards Rifle Division area, battalion commander A. G. Balutkin from 28th Guards Rifle Regiment was killed, but the ridgeline opposite was rapidly taken. The divisional commander wrote how a German 75mm battery on the western slope of the Malyy Karikvayvish fired on the advancing companies, but was forced to quickly cease firing by 122mm guns. The six guns were captured. The Soviet artillery commander was admonished for not having destroyed the battery in the opening bombardment. The 24th Guards Regiment in the south was not doing very well, as the 65th Rifle Division was being held in front of Bolshoi Karikvayvish. The commander, V. Lazarev, wanted to stop the advance, but was ordered to push on through the saddle between the hills to assist 65th Rifle Division by threatening the rear of Venediger. Korneyev's battalion from 24th Guards Regiment was used to dissuade enemy attacks from Venediger. The 35th Guards Rifle Regiment in reserve moved forward to the Titovka with a company from the 1st Separate Guards Sapper Battalion.

The reports written by the German commanders described the Soviet attacks in more detail. In area Karl at 0810 hrs, three Soviet companies moved on Trichterhöhe from the south and west. Leutnant Carrer,

The veteran 10th Guards Rifle Division attacked either side of the Katschberg. The 14th Rifle Division followed behind; it crossed the Titovka and broke into the area bordering the two Gebirgs divisions. Advancing to the north-west, they pressed onto the Russian Road to get behind the Litsa front line. Soviet infantry were prolifically armed with semi-automatic weapons, including the PPSh-41 submachine gun and SVT-40 rifle. In particular, naval infantry brigades had separate submachine-gun companies. Here, Soviet infantry move forward in typical summer Arctic terrain that had few trees. (Nik Cornish at www.Stavka.org.uk)

the leader of 13.Kompanie, ordered a retreat to Katschberg, and heavy fire was experienced; most NCOs were lost and the company fought their way towards Isarlager; they met a *Zug* from 7./Gebirgsjäger-Regiment 137 behind position Kathrein. The combined force retreated in bounds, sometimes finding good defensive positions to keep their pursuers at bay. Their retreat was going to have to change course, as by 0800 hrs, Soviet soldiers were in the north-west section of Katschberg; by 1000 hrs, two permanent bunkers had been destroyed and the eastern portion of the base vacated; the *Infanterie-Geschütze* were

The superiority of the Soviets in artillery would be on display in the offensive; however, the difficulties of moving the guns would limit their effectiveness. Here, the Soviets are resorting to hauling a 45mm gun up a hill. This calibre of gun would be used to fire on the embrasures of bunkers. (TASS via Getty Images)

also destroyed and the mortar unit wiped out. The 3.Zug of 7./Gebirgsjäger-Regiment 137 in their trench was holding the Soviets 20m away.

The Katschberg position was thought to be lost, and Stuka dive-bombers attacked the position in the evening. A small garrison of artillery crew, soldiers from Gebirgsjäger-Regiment 137 and pioneers commanded by Hauptmann Kohlert survived the bombardment at 1800 hrs. Then they moved out at night to Camp Haller with their wounded; 40 men reached the camp that night. Other small groups were detached and took their chances in evading through Soviet lines to the Titovka. Two soldiers encountered a Soviet unit preparing to attack. Before they were recognized as German, they took coats from dead Soviet soldiers and joined with the Soviet unit in advancing toward the German positions. Their disguise was successful, but the Soviet attack was not: it failed to break the German line and the two German soldiers played dead in front of the positions. When the Soviets withdrew, the two soldiers slipped off the coats and reached friendly positions. Many such expedients were taken by those cut off to reach their own lines.

Elsewhere that morning, a Soviet battalion moved north of Katschberg and south of Araberberg. The position occupied by 8./Gebirgsjäger-Regiment 137 in Araberberg was vacated by 0930 hrs, with the garrison moving to the position Schwarzer Grat (Black Ridge). Oberleutnant Ziese from II./Gebirgsjäger-Regiment 137 received orders to establish a defensive position there and defend it against the Soviets pushing from the Katschberg area; this assisted Strachwitz at Isarlager, but the positions of I./Gebirgs-Artillerie-Regiment 111 east of his location were occupied by two Soviet companies and three tanks were seen on the Araberweg. In the evening, Hauptmann Junker at Schwarzer Grat was listed as missing whilst repelling a Soviet attack. The position there moved back 200m, and was reinforced by elements of II./Gebirgsjäger-Regiment 136. Isarlager was for the moment safe.

Further north, at Tartarenkopf north a Soviet battalion was pushed back and moved

The artillery bombardment prior to the start of the offensive was impressive, but German fortifications were built to withstand the shells from the Soviet 76mm divisional gun seen here. (The Dmitri Baltermants Collection/Corbis via Getty Images)

OPPOSITE

1. 7 October: 10th Guards Rifle Division elements attack 13./Gebirgsjäger-Regiment 137 in Trichterhöhe and Katschberg. Both depleted garrisons move to Hallerlager.

2. 7 October: Tarterenkopf Süd and Nord are enveloped. Late morning, Soviets begin to cross the Titovka River north of the Laja See.

3. 7 October, 0950 hrs: Soviets reach the Titovka. The positions of I./Gebirgs-Artillerie-Regiment 111 are captured, and Hauptmann Junker forms positions on the Schwarzer Grat. Reinforcements from II./Gebirgsjäger-Regiment 136 arrive.

4. 7/8 October: Venediger is attacked from the north-west, and the garrison retreats to Rainerlager.

5. 7/8 October: Zuckerhütl is surrounded, and the garrison evacuates to Rainerlager.

6. 7 October, Ortler holds its positions, then retreats to Rainerlager.

7. 7/8 October: Vevi and Veronika are bypassed, and the Soviets move on Jagdlager.

8. Evening, 8 October: Rainerlager is evacuated and the bridge destroyed. 6./Gebirgs-Artillerie-Regiment 111 accompanies I./Gebirgsjäger-Regiment 137 to Nialla height 328.1.

9. 8 October: Isarlager is attacked by aircraft in the morning and by artillery in the afternoon. The Schwarzer Grat positions hold. II./Gebirgsjäger-Regiment 136 is ordered to retreat from Isarlager at 1850 hrs, followed by III./Gebirgsjäger-Regiment 136 and II./Gebirgsjäger-Regiment 137 at 2000 hrs. The bridge is destroyed.

10. 8 October: The 2nd Battalion of 28th Guards Rifle Regiment builds a temporary bridge across the Titovka. The III./Gebirgsjäger-Regiment 137 is ordered to stop them interdicting the road. Waitzer retreats and joins up with his battalion; they observe Soviets advancing towards the Lanhöhe and Hauptmann Dorn immediately attacks.

past the base to the back of Tartarenkopf south by 0910 hrs; this persuaded Oberleutnant Waitzer to withdraw his *Kompanie* 400m from Tartarenkopf north to a ridge named Perserkogel. From here Soviet attacks that morning were held, but the Soviets used the cover of a snow storm to cross the Titovka south of the Laja See. Waitzer decided to retreat, and reached other elements of his battalion on the Lanweg at km 16.

The situation further south was slightly better. At Venediger, the Soviet artillery bombardment caused heavy damage to the trench system, minefields and wire. A Soviet attack was repelled at 0945 hrs. Heavy artillery fire was brought on the base throughout the day; the north-west area of the base was attacked unsuccessfully at 1900 hrs. At Ortler, the commander, Hauptmann Binder, became a casualty whilst leading a counter-attack that threw a Soviet platoon out of the camp at 1645 hrs; despite the base being completely surrounded, the wire was keeping most of the Soviets out. Instead of giving these bases their full attention, the Soviets went around them to approach Vevi and Veronika. Indeed, they pushed past these two positions and moved on Kaminhöhe and Jagdlager. Deflected again by Major Thiele's attack with 13./Gebirgsjäger-Regiment 136 on the morning of 8 October, the Soviets headed to Isarlager. The III./Gebirgsjäger-Regiment 136 had begun to arrive the previous night, and Walitschek's 13./Gebirgsjäger-Regiment 136 advanced to relieve Thiele's 8./Gebirgs-Artillerie-Regiment 111 on Kaminhöhe at Jagdlager. The I./Radfahr-Aufklärungs-Brigade Norwegen also moved into position along the Titovka. On the morning of 8 October, air raids on Isarlager occurred. In the afternoon, minor attacks were made on the Schwarzer Grat; instead, the focus was on targeting Isarlager with artillery.

On the night of 8 October, the garrison of Ortler was free to disengage. Around 100 of the 300 in the camp were casualties. Only 40 men were combat ready, as the others were looking after the wounded. Leutnant Jahn, a paymaster, commanded the retreat. In order to deceive the Soviets, they initially retreated towards Isarlager. They altered course and crossed the Titovka 1km north of Rainerlager. They headed towards Lan Hill, but found they were in between two sets of attacking Soviet forces. They had no choice but to storm up a slope, next to the Soviets, and were shot at from both sides. Most were killed or wounded just before reaching safety. The remainder made their way to the Nialla Massiv on 9 October, where they met with I./Gebirgsjäger-Regiment 137 that evening.

In the south, on 7 October, Zuckerhutl and Rabenkopf had received the attention of a battalion each of Soviet soldiers. In the late morning, the wire at Zuckerhutl prevented them from entering the base; by 1600 hrs, the base was reported almost completely surrounded. The Germans stated that the Soviets, without fear of loss, used cover provided by folds in the ground to approach close to the wire to cut openings. The garrison observed guns being brought forward. The complexity of the trench system was keeping casualties low, despite heavy bombardment and close combat. A machine-gun *Zug* located at Rainerlager was used to keep open a passage to the rear slope of Rabenkopf. Retreating soldiers from other areas of the line were gathered at the Titovka and readied for a counter-attack from Rainerlager. At 2000 hrs, Zuckerhutl reported camp fires 4–5km to the south-west; the Soviets were going around their position. In the late evening, the divisional commander ordered Neuburg to withdraw the Zuckerhutl garrison to Rainerlager; this was completed by 0400 hrs on 8 October without interference. That morning,

Crossing the Titovka River, 8/9 October 1944

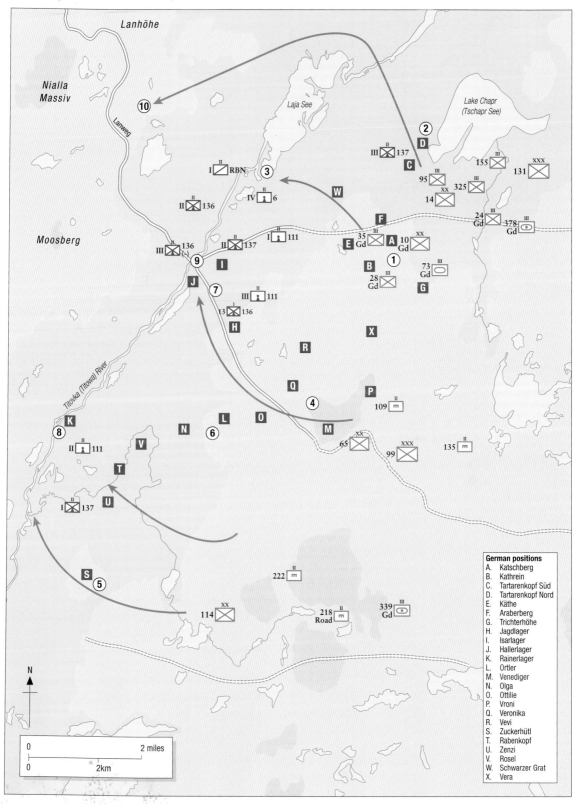

German positions
A. Katschberg
B. Kathrein
C. Tartarenkopf Süd
D. Tartarenkopf Nord
E. Käthe
F. Araberberg
G. Trichterhöhe
H. Jagdlager
I. Isarlager
J. Hallerlager
K. Rainerlager
L. Ortler
M. Venediger
N. Olga
O. Ottilie
P. Vroni
Q. Veronika
R. Vevi
S. Zuckerhütl
T. Rabenkopf
U. Zenzi
V. Rosel
W. Schwarzer Grat
X. Vera

The 2nd Battalion of the 28th Guards Regiment reached the Titovka late on 8 October, and, seizing many horse-drawn carts loaded with straw, made an emergency bridge over the river near the Laja See, a lake-type extension of the Titovka. That night, the mortars, already firing at long range, were brought forward. (Courtesy of the Central Museum of the Armed Forces, Moscow via Stavka)

the Soviets were seen crossing the Titovka south-west of Rainerlager. The garrison of Venediger reached Rainerlager at the same time, assisted by a *Zug* from 1./Gebirgsjäger-Regiment 137 sent out to rendezvous with them. Rabenkopf was holding out, but the commander of II./Gebirgs-Artillerie-Regiment 111 reported the Soviets had occupied Zuckerhutl and were marching straight to Rainerlager with 150 men. At 1700 hrs, Degen ordered Neuburg to move from Rainerlager to Moosberg. At 2100 hrs, the garrison gathered on the west bank, and just prior to setting off, a *Zug* from Radfahr-Aufklärungs-Brigade Norwegen and 6./Gebirgs-Artillerie-Regiment 111 arrived to join them. The bridge was blown, and by the morning, Neuburg had reached the Nialla Massiv.

Isarlager guarded the bridge over the Titovka. Clerical staff, baggage train and medical facilities were located here. Those isolated from their units were making their way there, seeking refuge. Wounded were being taken to the camp. The camp commander, Hauptmann Strachwitz, organized the defences. He put together temporary units and moved them into the front line. Baggage handlers and clerical staff formed the reserve. The SS artillery battery was ordered to the bank of the Titovka. Camp Haller was close by, but on 8 October, the Soviets had infiltrated between the two camps and pushed on to the Titovka. Four-barrelled 20mm guns commanded by Feldwebel Hoffmann opened an intensive fire against the Soviets once they were detected in the scrub close to the camp perimeter.

Crossing the Tundra

Major Kondrashov's 1st Battalion of 70th Naval Rifle Brigade (127th Light Rifle Corps) was told about the new offensive on 5 October, and started to move the next day. Water obstacles had to be crossed at fords, as the building of pontoons would reveal the presence of 127th Light Rifle Corps to German aerial reconnaissance. No fires were lit, for the same reason. Pestanov (1976, p.99) reported that each soldier of 70th Naval Rifle Brigade had food for five days, a rifle or submachine gun with 1,500 rounds, and six hand grenades. The men and packhorses moved in an endless file. Food supplies and tents were dragged on sledges. On 7 October, their path led across swampy ground and the packhorses soon became stuck; the brigade had to detour 3km to the south, forcing them to march during the night over a layer of moss that had hardened as the temperature grew colder. The men slept on higher elevations side by side on damp ground covered by reindeer moss and thorny bushes. On 8 October, the Litsa River was crossed at a ford and they entered a swampy valley. Again, some horses could not manage. The overcast weather and gusty wind precluded German reconnaissance aircraft from flying. Then, on 9 October, they crossed the noisy Titovka River, up to their knees in cold water. They entered a zone of birch trees that could be used for kindling fires; otherwise, they had brought along their own wood. Boulder fields were more common, and many horses damaged their hooves on them. When the horses refused to cross the stony Petsamo River, the soldiers made hoof coverings out of tents. Once across, they went north, but by then had only a day's ration of bread and two kilograms of forage per horse. Even though they were not sure what the objective was, the Germans were aware the envelopment by the Light Rifle Corps was occurring, but no longer had the reserves to oppose the Soviet units moving through the tundra. Degen would have no other option but to commence a withdrawal.

The brigade commander Colonel Blak described the situation to Major-General Zhukov. The latter ordered the naval infantry to keep on moving, saying there was no food in the tundra. The sooner into the battle, the sooner their rescue was what he told the staff officers of the brigade. The march continued through into the night on the fourth day. A brief halt to sleep for three hours in the bitter cold was not that successful; the soldiers had to move to keep warm. Reconnaissance teams sent out ahead then found the main Petsamo–Salmijärvi road 3km in front of them. They moved out at 0200 hrs in rain, and crossed without detection.

After crossing the Petsamo River, the brigade was ordered to reinforce 126th Light Rifle Corps to block the enemy's retreat on the night of 13 October. A night march on 12 October was necessary. The following morning, exhaustion was leading many to fall asleep on the frozen ground; their commanders encouraged them not to. Two hours of rest was permitted before another move to the Tarnet Road.

Retreating from Isarlager

On the basis of the sparse intelligence available to Degen, his immediate reaction was to order a withdrawal from the Titovka. The river was to be defended until the night of 8/9 October, not only to gain time for the construction of a new defensive line but also to keep open the line of retreat for 6.Gebirgs-Division. The new defensive line would be south-east of Luostari. The guns from Luostari Airfield were to be brought forward in units of two 8.8cm guns and three 2cm guns. The forward positions were to be commanded by Oberstleutnant Otto Stampfer, the commander of Gebirgsjäger-Regiment 136. The rear positions were the responsibility of Major Grumm, the commander of Gebirgsjäger-Regiment 137.

At 1645 hrs on 8 October, the order to retreat from Isarlager was given, with the artillery leading. The II./Gebirgsjäger-Regiment 137 headed north-west towards the Nialla Massiv, with II./Gebirgsjäger-Regiment 136 moving north along the Lanweg. To attempt to clear the way, III./Gebirgsjäger-Regiment 137 (which earlier on had encountered 400 Soviets moving south of Laja See to the Lanweg) had fought a delaying action. They were only partially successful; by 1830 hrs, with the coherence of the battalion breaking up, they were also ordered to retreat along the Lanweg.

Meretskov was aware of the German predicament and vulnerability of 6.Gebirgs-Division. Late on

Using a never-before deployed amount of firepower, the Soviets ruptured the German lines, capturing base Katschberg and encircling Venediger and Ortler. The garrisons of the strongpoints needed to fight through the encirclement to reach their own lines. The Gebirgs-Division had three battalions of 7.5cm guns that could be broken down and loaded onto mules. This gave them a chance of escaping the initial Soviet pursuit, providing they were not targeted by counter-battery fire. Many batteries, however, were recently moved forward of the Titovka River, and were caught before they could retreat to the river. (Nik Cornish at www.Stavka.org.uk)

A thick layer of snow fell on wet ground as 70th Naval Rifle Brigade began their march into the tundra, making a wide sweep that would go around Luostari and threaten the Arctic Ocean Highway. This method was, to Kraütler, an enticing prospect. He wrote that the Germans had used the same tactics, but the Soviets had more trained soldiers and material to make such a move achievable (Kraütler 1962, p. 406). The soldiers were carrying between 35 and 40kg each. The 76mm pack guns were brought forward on horses, as were 120mm mortars. Pack horses carried six mountain guns with 200 rounds, and 24 mortars with 420 rounds. Horses had a 130kg and reindeer a 35kg load of ammunition. Horses frequently lost their footing, but the reindeer had no such difficulties. (Nik Cornish at www.Stavka.org.uk)

8 October, he ordered 131st Rifle Corps to capture Luostari and reinforced them with 368th Rifle Division from 99th Rifle Corps. The capture of Luostari would open the route to Petsamo. The settlement lay astride the Arctic Ocean Highway and provided access to the Nikel Road. From here the Soviets could threaten a move north to Petsamo to encircle the Litsa front, or move south and threaten the Lappland Army retreating from Finland. The 10th Guards Rifle Division was given to 99th Rifle Corps, as defensive positions east of the Titovka were resisting and interfering with road building. The 65th Rifle Division was ordered to destroy these positions whilst other units of 99th Rifle Corps pushed further across the river. The weather was good on 9 October and would enable the air force to fly close air support and interdiction. The Germans would also fly, but only 200 sorties were flown, with unspecified results.

On the night of 8 October, Hauptmann Ruepp's II./Gebirgsjäger-Regiment 136 had reached the Lanweg at kilometre 18. One machine-gun *Zug* from 9./Gebirgsjäger-Regiment 136 was tasked with securing the retreat of Hauptmann Förschl's III./Gebirgsjäger-Regiment 136 from Isarlager; one *Zug* of 7./Gebirgsjäger-Regiment 136 and the pioneer platoon from 10.Kompanie was sent to the Radfahr-Aufklärungs-Brigade Norwegen; and one *Zug* of 6./Gebirgsjäger-Regiment 16 was sent on to reconnoitre the Lanweg further north. Some machine guns were not available because they were lost in previous engagements. The baggage train was sent ahead with 8./Gebirgsjäger-Regiment 136 following, then 7.Kompanie (one *Zug*), 9.Kompanie (minus two machine-gun *Züge*) 10.Kompanie (minus the pioneer *Zug*) and 6.Kompanie (minus one *Zug* plus one *Zug* from 9.Kompanie). The battalion staff personnel were behind 8.Kompanie. The march started at 2030 hrs. The baggage train reported the hill north-east and north-west of kilometre 16 was occupied by the enemy. Hauptmann Schleppe with his 8.Kompanie and the *Zug* from 7.Kompanie reinforced by a heavy machine-gun *Gruppe* were launched against the position, but were repelled. The extent of the enemy positions was difficult to determine in the dark. Reinforced by 6.Kompanie and mortars, the second attack was successful. The baggage train took cover at the foot of a cliff whilst the combat units led on the road. At 2245 hrs, a Soviet counter-attack from hills to the north caused severe losses, as the Germans had limited ammunition. Oberfeldwebel Kendlbacher found ammunition and renewed the attack, pushing the Soviets from the heights overlooking the road. Förschl's III./Gebirgsjäger-Regiment 136 was following, and hearing the noise of fighting ahead, diverted south of the Lanweg. He succeeded in extricating his unit to the Lanhöhe (Lan Hill).

The Soviets, especially the Naval Infantry brigades, relied on 82mm and 120mm mortars for their fire support. These could be loaded onto mules and horses. Here, 82mm mortars are shown. (Courtesy of the Central Museum of the Armed Forces, Moscow via Stavka)

Ruepp's radio contact with the regiment was lost when the withdrawal began. At 0130 hrs on 9 October, his battalion was split into individual combat groups because the darkness and enemy action meant keeping the soldiers together in their own *Kompanien* was impracticable. These groups were ordered to move independently. Soviet soldiers speaking German tried to entice them to move forward into the fire zone. The baggage train's vehicles with the badly wounded were packed together on the road and suffered severe losses as machine-gun fire clattered into them from the surrounding hills. The front company immediately attacked to free the road but the extent of the enemy positions was difficult to determine in the dark. The battalion was intermingled with artillery crew, Radfahr soldiers and horse handlers. Wagons from the baggage train and vehicles from the SS artillery unit were destroyed by enemy fire. The attack failed and losses were heavy amongst the baggage train in particular.

At 0600 hrs, Leutnant Scholl, the leader of 6.Kompanie, with about 80 men and the baggage train made a diversion south-west on the old Lanweg road. The wagons had to be destroyed, as the road could not take them. The horses were untied and hitched to some two-wheeled carts. Scholl reached Luostari, and leaving the baggage train there, reported to Ruepp at Lanweg kilometre 7.5. The rest of the battalion had fought through to kilometre 12.5 in the morning, as with the light the enemy ceased further attacks. Forming two temporary platoons with machine-gun and mortar support, the battalion had the combat power to force their way through positions near the Lanhöhe between 0900 and 1000 hrs. Ruepp criticized the Radfahr units' motivation and wrote that they were a hindrance rather than help; his losses were nine dead, 30 wounded, and 157 missing. Förschl's III./Gebirgsjäger-Regiment 136 was following and, hearing the noise of fighting ahead, diverted south of the Lanweg. He succeeded in extricating his unit to the Lanhöhe.

Strachwitz, the commander of II./Gebirgsjäger-Regiment 137, was the last to leave the camp. His men were subjected to machine-gun and mortar fire as they crossed the Titovka, but the Soviets did not launch a pursuit. They reached I./Radfahr-Aufklärungs-Brigade Norwegen on both banks of the river and joined with the garrison of the Venediger camp that had also escaped to the river; they then started to make their way to the Nialla

Two-wheeled carts were the only means that could transit the Old Lanweg. Four-wheeled carts had to be ditched in favour of the two-wheeled variant when the baggage train of II./Gebirgs-Jäger-Regiment 136 had to retreat along the Old Lanweg. (Martin Sachse/Ullstein Bild via Getty Images)

Massiv. Pioneers of Pionier-Bataillon 82 destroyed the bridge in Isarlager. When Strachwitz reached the heights, and at the moment he had brought the men entrusted to him to safety, he was hit by a bullet, but only wounded. His determined actions had stopped the camp from being overrun and prevented total chaos. He was nominated for the Knight's Cross. The 38th and 311th Rifle regiments of 65th Rifle Division crossed at fording sites south of the destroyed bridge at 0500 hrs on 9 October.

The Lanhöhe

The struggle for Lanhöhe, part of a broad, bulky range of hills that together with the Nialloaivi hill to the south-east of Luostari represented a last defensive line preventing a breakthrough into the broad valley of Luostari, started on 9 October. The Radfahr-Aufklärungs-Brigade Norwegen unit occupied the north side of Lanhöhe. The reconnaissance battalion of Hauptmann Haueisen was on Suaionaivi Hill that was on the other side of marshland further north. Artillerymen in company strength deployed as infantry, commanded by Hauptman Burger-Schiedlin, were placed with the Radfahr brigade. Some 7.5cm anti-tank guns were in position on the road, and Soviet tanks were unable to go off-road through the marshy or rocky terrain.

On 9 October, 35th Guards Rifle Regiment, having crossed the river south of the Laja See and established a bridgehead 1.5–2km deep and 2.5–3km wide, threatened to envelop Isarlager to the south. The 28th Guards Rifle Regiment was tasked with cutting the road 1.5–2km north-west of the bridge to stop German reserves brought forward on the Lanweg from reaching the bridge; that night, two battalions attacked the Germans there. The divisional command post detected the enemy 200m from their position, and the submachine-gun company of 35th Guards Rifle Regiment, commanded by Captain A. P. Shulyayev's men, counter-attacked; Shulyayev was killed during this engagement.

Hauptmann Köhnen's III./Gebirgsjäger-Regiment 137, having fought to keep the Lanweg clear on 8 October, had the same role the following day. The Lanhöhe was being attacked by two battalions and the Soviets were beginning to advance from Isarlager. In the late morning, III./Gebirgsjäger-Regiment 137 had 11.Kompanie and 13.Kompanie in the front line 300m east of the junction of the old Lanweg with the new Lanweg. Wire was laid to facilitate communications with battalion headquarters. At 1615 hrs, seven Soviet tanks were observed moving along the Lanweg from the south, with about 120 infantry on board. At 1645 hrs, 13.Kompanie, according to the battalion commander, destroyed two tanks in close combat and the tank attack was driven off; the loss of the tanks may be better attributed to the presence of the *Pak Zug* of 16./Gebirgsjäger-Regiment 137. The battalion radioed for machine-gun and mortar ammunition. By 2130 hrs, 13.Kompanie had to move back to the Lanweg to prevent a Soviet advance going round their flank. During the night, snowfall had created ground cover, and 12.Kompanie soldiers were committed to hold the line against strengthening Soviet probes. As the Soviets advanced onto the Lanhöhe, the battalion had to move closer to the feature to support a counter-attack from further west along the road. The following morning, Leutnant Carrer was wounded and replaced by a Feldwebel. The divisional commander, Degen, was reportedly briefed in person about the situation.

After midnight on 9/10 October, the Soviets penetrated north of the Lanhöhe with two to three companies and pushed to Lanweg kilometre 9. At 0300 hrs, the Soviets attacked the Lanhöhe and pushed Radfahr-Aufklärungs-Brigade Norwegen from the hill. The tractors from the SS artillery battery helped to evacuate some badly wounded soldiers, but others were lost to the attack. The staff doctor stayed behind. The report from III./Gebirgsjäger-Regiment 137 then prompted the formation of a *Kampfgruppe* from II./Gebirgsjäger-Regiment 136 and regimental staff commanded by Hauptmann Schöll at kilometre 8. Stampfer was tasked with regaining the Lanhöhe on the morning of 10 October. All the elements of Gebirgsjäger-Regiments 136 and 137 with pioneers, artillerymen and cyclists that could be gathered together in time attacked the hill. A light covering of snow that had fallen the previous night was on the ground. From kilometre 10, a counter-attack recaptured the southern part of the hill. The 13./Gebirgsjäger-Regiment 136 arrived, but their attack was hampered by poor co-ordination and led to friendly fire. Walitschek was killed leading his 13./Gebirgsjäger-Regiment 136. Hauptmann Hengl, with elements of II./Gebirgsjäger-Regiment 136, reached the hill. At 1530 hrs, Major Kuhnt, the commander of I./Grenadier-Brigade 193,

Snow cover was not a given in October, but did occur on some days, notably 9 October, especially on the Lanhöhe elevation, and later on in the month during the retreat to Nautsi. On these occasions in particular, the Jägers made the most of their camouflage smocks to provide concealment in terrain that did not always provide much natural cover. (Nik Cornish at www.Stavka.org.uk)

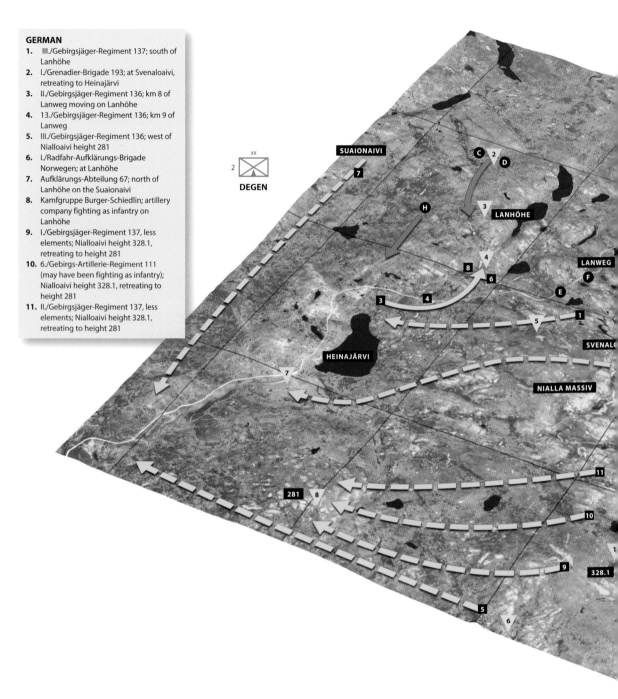

GERMAN

1. III./Gebirgsjäger-Regiment 137; south of Lanhöhe
2. I./Grenadier-Brigade 193; at Svenaloaivi, retreating to Heinajärvi
3. II./Gebirgsjäger-Regiment 136; km 8 of Lanweg moving on Lanhöhe
4. 13./Gebirgsjäger-Regiment 136; km 9 of Lanweg
5. III./Gebirgsjäger-Regiment 136; west of Nialloaivi height 281
6. I./Radfahr-Aufklärungs-Brigade Norwegen; at Lanhöhe
7. Aufklärungs-Abteilung 67; north of Lanhöhe on the Suaionaivi
8. Kamfgruppe Burger-Schiedlin; artillery company fighting as infantry on Lanhöhe
9. I./Gebirgsjäger-Regiment 137, less elements; Nialloaivi height 328.1, retreating to height 281
10. 6./Gebirgs-Artillerie-Regiment 111 (may have been fighting as infantry); Nialloaivi height 328.1, retreating to height 281
11. II./Gebirgsjäger-Regiment 137, less elements; Nialloaivi height 328.1, retreating to height 281

▼ EVENTS

1. 9/10 October: I./Gebirgsjäger-Regiment 137 with elements of II./Gebirgsjäger-Regiment 137 (Venediger garrison), elements of 16./Gebirgsjäger-Regiment 137 and 6./Gebirgs-Artillerie-Regiment 111 defend Nialloaivi height 328.1.

2. Evening, 9/10 October: Two to three companies of the 325th Rifle Regiment advance north of the Lanhöhe and reach the Lanweg. I./Radfahr-Aufklärungs-Brigade Norwegen on the Lanhöhe retreats.

3. Morning, 10 October: Hauptmann Schöll from Gebirgsjäger-Regiment 136 regimental staff and II./Gebirgsjäger-Regiment 136 elements commanded by Hauptmann Hengl that succeeded in retreating on the night of 8/9 October join with the Radfahr-Aufklärungs-Brigade Norwegen soldiers and recapture the southern part of the Lanhöhe. Elements from the 24th Guards Rifle Regiment have reinforced the 325th Rifle Regiment elements on the height.

4. Morning, 10 October: 13./Gebirgsjäger-Regiment 136 deploys against infiltrating Soviet units, but only when the weather clears are their attacks successful.

5. 10 October: III./Gebirgsjäger-Regiment 137, south of the Lanhöhe, having repelled attacks from 325th Rifle Regiment the previous day, sees off elements of the 10th Guards Rifle Division and then escapes on the old Lanweg.

6. 10 October: III./Gebirgsjäger-Regiment 136 on Koivunokka is attacked by the 114th Rifle Division with mortar support, and successfully counter-attacks them.

7. Morning, 11 October: I./Grenadier-Brigade 193 defends the Lanweg at Heinajärvi from 65th Rifle Division.

8. 11 October: I./Gebirgsjäger-Regiment 137 and 6./Gebirgs-Artillerie-Regiment 111 on height 281 repel attacks from 114th Rifle Division.

Note: gridlines are shown at intervals of 2km (1.24 miles)

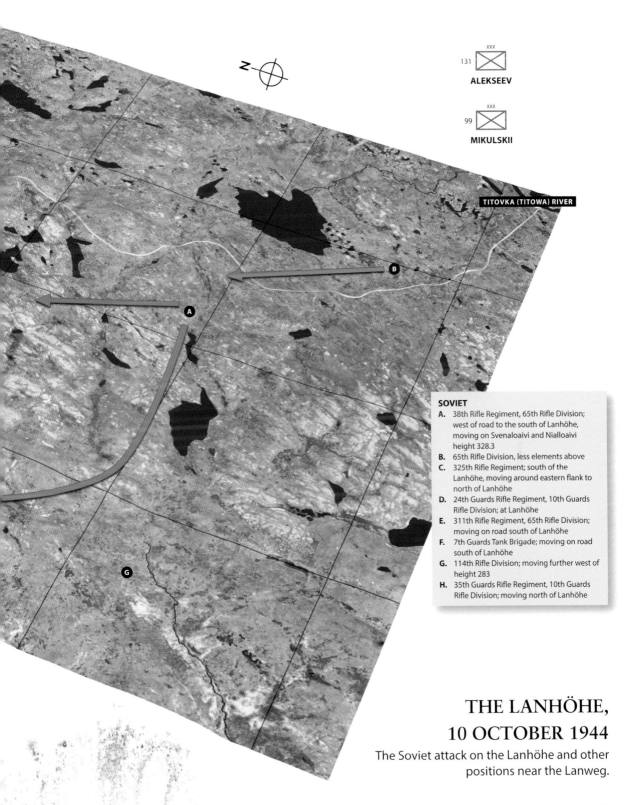

131 ⊠ XXX
ALEKSEEV

99 ⊠ XXX
MIKULSKII

TITOVKA (TITOWA) RIVER

B

A

G

SOVIET
A. 38th Rifle Regiment, 65th Rifle Division; west of road to the south of Lanhöhe, moving on Svenaloaivi and Nialloaivi height 328.3
B. 65th Rifle Division, less elements above
C. 325th Rifle Regiment; south of the Lanhöhe, moving around eastern flank to north of Lanhöhe
D. 24th Guards Rifle Regiment, 10th Guards Rifle Division; at Lanhöhe
E. 311th Rifle Regiment, 65th Rifle Division; moving on road south of Lanhöhe
F. 7th Guards Tank Brigade; moving on road south of Lanhöhe
G. 114th Rifle Division; moving further west of height 283
H. 35th Guards Rifle Regiment, 10th Guards Rifle Division; moving north of Lanhöhe

THE LANHÖHE,
10 OCTOBER 1944
The Soviet attack on the Lanhöhe and other positions near the Lanweg.

GEBIRGSJÄGER-REGIMENT 136 COUNTER-ATTACKS ON THE LANHÖHE (PP. 38–39)

On 9 October, the Soviets had captured the Lanhöhe elevation, and from here would be able to target the only road in the region – the Lanweg – that the Germans would have to use to retreat. Oberstleutnant Stampfer, the commander of Gebirgsjäger-Regiment 136, was tasked with regaining the Lanhöhe on the morning of 10 October. Hauptmann Walitschek with his 13.Kompanie of Gebirgsjäger-Regiment 136, reached the hill together with Hauptmann Hengl with elements of II.Battalion of the regiment.

Here, Walitschek and a patrol from 13./Gebirgsjäger-Regiment 136 prepares to ambush a mortar team from Generalov's company in the 35th Guards Rifle Regiment. Walitschek is on the right kneeling (**1**), armed with an MP 40 (**2**), and is giving instructions to a light machine-gun team. The soldier to the

right of Walitschek (**3**) has attached a rifle grenade, awaiting the order to pop up and fire at the Soviet mortar position (**4**). The machine-gunner (**5**) is behind a bush, ready to fire his MG34 (**6**) through the gorse. The soldier behind him is armed with a Gewehr 33/40 (**7**) and is bringing forward the machine-gun ammunition.

The Soviet mortar crew is unaware of Walitschek and his patrol. An observer (**8**) is shouting aiming corrections to the crew. Next to the mortar observer, a sniper is looking through the telescopic sight of his rifle (**9**), watching for German attackers that he thinks will approach from this direction.

Walitschek would be killed leading his company here, and Stampfer would be badly wounded, dying in the field hospital several days later.

was tasked with the leadership of the German forces around Lanhöhe because Oberstleutnant Stampfer was wounded. The 14th Rifle Division's 325th Rifle Regiment held important heights and helped stem the counter-attack. The Germans would vacate the hill on the night of 10 October.

At 1700 hrs on 10 October, to the south of the hill, the battalion commander of III./Gebirgsjäger-Regiment 137 relieved the 11. and 13. *Kompanien* with 12.Kompanie because they had suffered heavy casualties. That evening, with orders to withdraw, the battalion was able to move along the Lanweg to Luostari, and they would reach the river by the settlement at 0900 hrs on 12 October. They had expended 67,500 rifle and machine-gun rounds, 3,400 mortar rounds and 1,200 hand grenades. Wheeled transport was able to resupply them throughout the battle.

The Soviets could deploy mortars to the Lanhöhe, but ammunition (carried by hand) was scarce. The M1938 120mm mortar had a trailer on wheels. (The LIFE Picture Collection/ Getty Images)

Elsewhere on the night of 9/10 October, the Soviets launched a night attack on Suaionaivi that was beaten back by the reconnaissance battalion. The III./Gebirgsjäger-Regiment 136 on the right wing repelled a Soviet attack (which was preceded by a mortar barrage in battalion strength) by a counter-attack by two *Züge*. They had orders to withdraw that night, and succeeded in doing so without pressure from the enemy.

The Soviets had issues bringing forward support units. Mikulskii had reported that the armoured units supporting 65th Rifle Division were hindered by the lack of suitable roads. He ordered a road 10–12km long to be built by the morning of 10 October over the Bolshoi Karikvayvish to the Titovka by 20th Svirsk Motorized Assault Combat Engineer Brigade, supported by a regiment from 65th Rifle Division and 368th Rifle Division from the second echelon. This was the only road that could be built. On 10 October, Mikulskii's artillery units were in the firing positions they had occupied since the start of the offensive; the crews were placed on road-building duty, except 64 heavy guns that could fire to longer ranges and 70 guns of 76mm and 45mm calibre that could be moved forward. The 65th Rifle Division was put into the second echelon and given road-building duty. At the end of the day, the artillery was able to move over the Titovka and the two bridge sites prepared by the engineers.

The next day, the 38th and 311th Rifle regiments of 65th Rifle Division were given 73rd Separate Guards Heavy Tank Regiment and 378th Guards Heavy Self-Propelled Artillery Regiment to advance west of the Lanweg. By 0800 hrs, 13 gun and mortar regiments were in position over the Titovka, but only half (250–300 pieces) were available to support the infantry, as most had to deploy along 8km of road on from the bridge. The 10th Guards Rifle Division shifted to the north. The artillery was firing at grid squares and could not accurately target enemy positions. Despite the attack being delayed three hours that morning because of co-ordination issues, 38th Rifle Regiment seized Hill 283. The 7th Guards Tank Brigade and 339th Guards Heavy

Self-Propelled Artillery Regiment supported 311th Rifle Regiment along the Lanweg. The 114th Rifle Division headed towards the Petsamo River.

Nialla Massiv

On the right wing, at 0900 hrs on 9 October, Neuburg's battalion (I./Gebirgsjäger-Regiment 137), having retreated from Zacharias, had reached Nialloaivi height 328.1. On the morning of 9 October, the soldiers retreating from the Isarlager were bombed by Soviet aircraft; Generalmajor Mathias Krautler, commander of Divisionsstab z.b.V. 140 in northern Finland, stated that 20mm guns shot three down. Neuberg, worried about further attacks, wanted to disperse his men, but more were being incorporated into his group. Neuburg had his I./Gebirgsjäger-Regiment 137, but was without 2.Kompanie that was guarding Luostari Airfield. He also commanded the *Pionier-Zug* of III./Gebirgsjäger-Regiment 137, elements of II./Gebirgsjäger-Regiment 137, the *Pionier-Zug* of Radfahr-Aufklärungs-Brigade Norwegen, 6./Gebirgs-Artillerie-Regiment 111, a *Pak Zug* from 16./Gebirgsjäger-Regiment 137 and 4./Feld-Ersatz-Bataillon 111; in total, 942 men with 40 light machine guns, three 8cm mortars and 10 heavy machine guns. With no specific orders, he decided to hold the height. Then Grumm radioed an order to establish a *Kampfgruppe* and command of III./Gebirgsjäger-Regiment 137 was given to Hauptmann Dapra, the commander of 4./Gebirgsjäger-Regiment 137, the machine-gun *Kompanie*.

Neuburg had no communications with the other units of the *Kampfgruppe* or I./Grenadier-Brigade 193 on his flank, and had to rely on messengers. Attempts to form an integrated fire plan were hampered, and a 400–500m open area from II./Gebirgsjäger-Regiment 137 to I./Grenadier-Brigade 193 existed. There was no artillery support; a line from the forward observer to batteries further back could not be laid. Weak attacks were repelled during the day, but the next day, a Soviet mortar bombardment was more serious; an order to limit ammunition expenditure was given. By 1000 hrs on 10 October, the road connecting the German and Soviet main roads was built and engineers in 99th Rifle Corps area had completed two bridges and two fording sites; however, the road in the German area had to be repaired by the Soviets and supplies had to wait.

At 2130 hrs on 10 October, the order to withdraw was given, as the Soviets had deployed two battalions against them. Neuburg established when each unit was to move and to where. The following morning before daybreak, the battalion had reached Hill 281 and reconnoitred potential defensive positions. Losses on Hill 328.3 were low because the Soviets had not pushed hard during the day and let them slip away during the night with no pursuit launched.

Hill 281 was a vegetation-free, flat-topped massif that dominated the surrounding area. The slopes to the north, west and south fell off

The Soviets often had to attack steep terrain defended effectively by German positions that, to avoid being targeted by artillery and tanks, were sited on the reverse slope. (TASS via Getty Images)

steeply in parts, but to the east and south-east an extensive flat slope with many hollows occupied the main part of the hill. A kilometre to the west of the hill there was a smaller hill, thickly covered with bushes, and occupied by III./Gebirgsjäger-Regiment 136. From the south-west a thick birch wood pushed its way to within 800–1,000m of Hill 281. South-east and north-east there were higher heights from which the Soviets could observe Hill 281, but these were a long way off. The valleys surrounding the hill had marshes in places.

Neuburg thought the position unfavourable for defence for any length of time. He placed his men on the reverse slope 20–50m from the crest, and held back a reserve. He gave the Soviets the opportunity to approach the hill. The reverse position, though protecting the soldiers from enemy fire, needed soldiers with high morale and trust in their own capabilities; they knew the enemy could close unseen. Close combat was to be expected. The men were exhausted, but the commander thought they were capable of holding the position this way.

At 0700 hrs, the first enemy soldiers appeared from the birch wood. A forward observer waited until 0800 hrs, when there were enough of the enemy so as not to be wasteful of ammunition before he called down fire. Whilst the positions of the neighbouring battalion on the right were known, those of the battalion on the other side were not. At 1000 hrs, 16 enemy tanks tried to push through on the Lanweg. At 1030 hrs, a counter-attack against them led by the *Pionier-Zug* of III./Gebirgsjäger-Regiment 137 and a *Zug* from 16./Gebirgsjäger-Regiment 137 destroyed a tank and brought the enemy to a halt because the wreck blocked the road. From their static positions the tanks targeted the eastern part of the hill. In late morning, with a mortar barrage supporting them, Soviet infantry closed on the hill. Two to three companies reached the crest, but on the German right flank they could not approach the crest because of flanking fire from the height to the west. Ammunition supplies were low and were used at close range to force the Soviets off the crest. The rear slopes were shot at during the afternoon with indirect fire from mortars.

At 2000 hrs, a message from I./Grenadier-Brigade 193 could not be deciphered because two letters were missing. At 2200 hrs, a reconnaissance party from 1.Kompanie could not find whether III./Gebirgsjäger-Regiment 136 was holding on the right. Neuburg sent out another patrol. As he did not have radio communications, he was unsure how long he should hold Hill 281. He distributed a withdrawal plan to the company commanders. At 0030 hrs on 12 October, the patrol returned and reported the neighbouring unit was no longer in position. With light machine guns having only 50 rounds each, at 0140 hrs Neuburg ordered a withdrawal. At 0225 hrs, in two groups, the battalion moved out to Erlöserberg, where the regimental staff was located. Moving in line through terrain with no paths, the unit reached the Lanweg at kilometre 6 and passed an enemy campfire 50m

The resistance of 2.Gebirgs-Division thwarted a Soviet breakthrough. Their defensive battle on the Titovka and Nialla Massiv was of the utmost importance to gain time for the retreat of 6.Gebirgs-Division further north. Generalmajor Mathias Kraütler wrote how each day and every hour that the Soviets could be prevented from gaining the Arctic Road network brought freedom and life to hundreds and thousands of their comrades in the north. (Nik Cornish at www. Stavka.org.uk)

The Soviet Air Force often compensated for the lack of artillery support the infantry would experience. The lack of roads would severely hamper the artillery's deployment to firing positions closer to the German line. The Soviets used a bomber division to attack the airfields that the Luftwaffe used. (Courtesy of the Central Museum of the Armed Forces, Moscow via Stavka)

distant. To make faster progress, a double line was adopted. The wounded slowed down the column. At 0500 hrs, the Erlöserberg was found abandoned. Neuburg pressed on towards the bridge, and found it burning and destroyed at 0600 hrs. A temporary bridge built near the wreckage was used to cross the river, as was a ford. German mortars targeted them, thinking they were Soviets, but caused no losses. By 0800 hrs, the battalion was on the west bank of the Petsamo River. Losses were 19 dead, 58 wounded and 10 missing.

The I./Gebirgsjäger-Regiment 137 on the Nialla Massiv and the reconnaissance battalion on the Suaionaivi had to hold their positions to enable a defensive line to form on the east bank of the Petsamo. Neuburg had repulsed attacks in close combat but the reconnaissance battalion Aufklärungs-Abteilung 67 commanded by Hauptmann Hauesian was less successful, as tanks advanced on the Lanweg and threatened to surround their positions. The order to evacuate was given.

Hauptmann Rüf, with 400 men, was caught in a basin and experienced fire from numerous sides. Rüf took charge and with the leading company advanced on the hill to the north to make a detour around the Soviet positions. He snatched the hill from the Soviets and strode through a long chain of lakes in a narrow area before the enemy reacted. In the darkness, Rüf on a large massif formed his men in all-round defence and then moved off towards Luostari with his shock troops in front. Fires and explosions lit the way. Degen was discussing the situation with his senior commanders when Rüf arrived in the Petsamo position.

On 12 October, the 24th and 35th Guards Rifle regiments of 10th Guards Rifle Division would cross the Petsamo River 2km north-east of Luostari. The 28th Guards Rifle Regiment with elements of 65th Rifle Division entered Luostari. The 114th Rifle Division was beginning to cross the Namajoki to the south-east of Luostari.

Advance to Luostari

Jodl reported that the Arctic Ocean Highway was blocked at kilometre 496 by 10 October. The 2./Aufklärungs-Abteilung 112 and II./Radfahr-Aufklärungs-Brigade Norwegen advanced along the road to kilometres 491 and 497, respectively. The 126th Light Rifle Corps had begun to advance onwards to Luostari Airfield. Förschl with III./Gebirgsjäger-Regiment 136 kept them in check. In the Petsamo Valley, Hengl with II./Gebirgsjäger-Regiment 136 covered the defensive positions. The I./Gebirgsjäger-Regiment 137 had to fight their way to the river and use an emergency bridge that was built by Hauptmann Flachberger under the burning bridge. The Soviets, having captured Erlöserberg, had a clear view of the retreating Germans and placed artillery on the position. Neuburg with 3. and 4./Feld-Ersatz-Bataillon 111 had 653 men with 40 light machine guns, two heavy machine guns, eight 8cm mortars and two IG guns. Hauptmann Weckerle's

Luostari and Petsamo, 12–15 October 1944

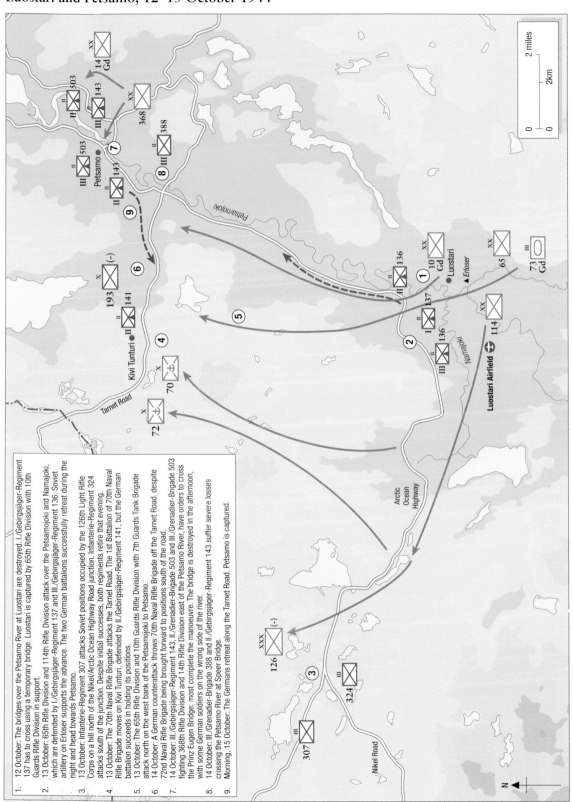

1. 12 October: The bridges over the Petsamo River at Luostari are destroyed. I./Gebirgsjäger-Regiment 137 has to cross using a temporary bridge. Luostari is captured by 65th Rifle Division with 10th Guards Rifle Division in support.
2. 13 October: 65th Rifle Division and 114th Rifle Division attack over the Petsamojoki and Namajoki, which are defended by I./Gebirgsjäger-Regiment 137 and III./Gebirgsjäger-Regiment 136. Soviet artillery on Erfoser supports the advance. The two German battalions successfully retreat during the night and head towards Petsamo.
3. 13 October: Infanterie-Regiment 307 attacks Soviet positions occupied by the 126th Light Rifle Corps on a hill north of the Nikel/Arctic Ocean Highway Road junction. Infanterie-Regiment 324 attacks south of the junction. Despite initial successes, both regiments retire that evening.
4. 13 October: The 70th Naval Rifle Brigade attacks the Tarnet Road. The 1st Battalion of 70th Naval Rifle Brigade moves on Kivi Tunturi, defended by II./Gebirgsjäger-Regiment 141, but the German battalion succeeds in holding its positions.
5. 13 October: The 65th Rifle Division and 10th Guards Rifle Division with 7th Guards Tank Brigade attack north on the west bank of the Petsamojoki to Petsamo.
6. 14 October: A German counterattack throws 70th Naval Rifle Brigade off the Tarnet Road, despite 72nd Naval Rifle Brigade being brought forward to positions south of the road.
7. 14 October: III./Gebirgsjäger-Regiment 143, II./Grenadier-Brigade 503 and III./Grenadier-Brigade 503 fighting 368th Rifle Division and 14th Rifle Division east of the Petsamo River, have orders to cross the Prinz Eugen Bridge; most complete the manoeuvre. The bridge is destroyed in the afternoon, with some German soldiers on the wrong side of the river.
8. 14 October: III./Grenadier-Brigade 388 and II./Gebirgsjäger-Regiment 143 suffer severe losses crossing the Petsamo River at Speer Bridge.
9. Morning, 15 October: The Germans retreat along the Tarnet Road. Petsamo is captured.

45

By 1600 hrs on 12 October, 73rd Separate Guards Heavy Tank Regiment had reached Luostari, but was halted by the Petsamo River as the bridges had been destroyed by the retreating Germans. Scouts were sent out to find a fording site, but the tanks were 30–50m above the river and the slope was 30 degrees. With the turret located around to the rear, the tank moved over the edge and shut off its engine. Sliding down the slope the tank entered the river. Once on the other side, rocks and branches were laid in front of the tracks to assist movement. (Courtesy of the Central Museum of the Armed Forces, Moscow via Stavka)

2./Gebirgsjäger-Regiment 137 with 3./Feld-Ersatz-Bataillon 111 were positioned north of the Namajoki River with III./Gebirgsjäger-Regiment 136 further west along the Luostari Road, and II./Gebirgsjäger-Regiment 136 was further north on the Arctic Ocean Highway. The bulk of I./Gebirgsjäger-Regiment 137 was at the road junction; 4./Gebirgsjäger-Regiment 137 was with Gebirgsjäger-Regiment 136.

On the night of 12/13 October, the Soviets crossed the river near the destroyed bridge. The river was fordable in numerous places. The area the Germans were occupying was hilly with bushes, ditches, gorges and crevices that provided good cover but made observation difficult, especially on the west to east axis. The Soviet attack started on the morning of 13 October at 0315 hrs, with two companies moving on 1./Gebirgsjäger-Regiment 137 on the Arctic Ocean Highway. At 0700 hrs, Neuburg brought 3./Gebirgsjäger-Regiment 137 forward and co-ordinated with Weckerle, also being attacked to the south. The danger was that the Soviets could cross the Namajoki and cut the Luostari Road. The 1. and 2./Gebirgsjäger-Regiment 137 pushed back the Soviet advance, but the enemy was free to regroup where the rivers met as the Germans had as yet no artillery. Then, a forward observer appeared and targeted the destroyed bridge sites by firing at map references. The Soviets replied with guns on the Erlöserberg and tanks on the Lanweg. The Germans were unable to move because of this fire. At 1230 hrs, 3./Gebirgsjäger-Regiment 137 was positioned in between I./Gebirgsjäger-Regiment 137 and II./Gebirgsjäger-Regiment 136; lack of communications made Neuburg worry for the integrity of his unit and their ability to report the presence of the enemy. At 1500 hrs, there was noise to the south where Weckerle was attacked. Neuburg sent two *Züge* from 4.Kompanie to assist him; the officer leading them was a casualty, but the Soviet advance was pushed back.

Two 15cm guns fired at Soviet tanks approaching the river. Förschl had counter-attacked some infantry that crossed the river, but was thrown back. He occupied a rounded hilltop where the Nikel Road met the Arctic Ocean Highway, but was thrown off; he had recaptured the feature, but was again repelled. These efforts were giving time for a defensive line to be established by Grenadier-Brigade 193 halfway between Luostari and the Speer Bridge. At 1550 hrs, Neuburg met with Förschl and they realized a retreat was needed, but by 1700 hrs, the Soviets had managed to get around their positions and there was nowhere to retreat to. They reported the situation to the regimental commander of Gebirgsjäger-Regiment 136 and were told to stand and re-organize. At 2200 hrs, a captured German soldier used a loudspeaker to incite the Germans to surrender. At midnight, Neuburg was at last permitted to retreat; his battalion slipped away and by 0230 hrs on 14 October, was marching towards Petsamo. The Soviets did not pursue. Losses to Neuburg's unit were 22 dead, 95 wounded and 50 missing.

Meanwhile, at the road junction west of Luostari, the Germans had begun to attack. On 10 October, Infanterie-Regiment 307 and 324 with supporting units had begun a motorized march north from Rovaniemi, a 400km journey. They were to defend the approaches to the Arctic Ocean Highway and the Nikel Road further south. The defence of the Nikel Road was more important than the Arctic Ocean Highway because the latter had to pass south of Salmijärvi on its way to Ivalo. The Soviets could interdict this passage if they broke through the defences at Nikel. South of the Nikel Road there were numerous barren hills and then barren tundra with neither trees nor roads. Further north, the Arctic Ocean Highway went through lakes and swamps to Luostari. Trees were stunted and widely spaced with dense brush. Infanterie-Regiment 307 with a light *Motorisiert* artillery battalion had positioned itself on the Arctic Ocean Highway, 14km south-west of Luostari. Infanterie-Regiment 324 with artillery, engineer and panzerjäger units was on the Nikel Road in support of Infanterie-Regiment 307. Both forces were not strong enough to hold their positions long, but Infanterie-Regiment 324 would soon be reinforced by SS-Infanterie-Bataillon 6 and two machine-gun battalions. Their objective was to delay the Soviets long enough to permit the Gebirgsjäger-Division to withdraw from Petsamo.

The 2.Gebirgs-Division had a night without alerts – a proper night's sleep. Most companies had lost a third of their strength, many had lost a half, but the Soviet plan to encircle them failed. The troops thought they were going to Kirkenes, but were disenchanted. They were sent back to defend the Arctic Ocean Road between Luostari and Ivalo in order to delay the Soviet pursuit and protect the German retreat of forces from Rovaniemi through Ivalo into Norway. (Nik Cornish at www.Stavka.org.uk)

On 12 October, Infanterie-Regiment 307 was given orders to attack a junction on the road to Luostari; but the regiment was attacked that night by 126th Light Rifle Corps, and the German attack was delayed until 13 October when the commander of Infanterie-Regiment 307 personally led his soldiers in the capture of Hill 175 near the road junction. The Light Rifle Corps had mortars and light guns but a massive counter-attack in the afternoon by a reinforcing Soviet unit threw the Germans off the hill. Infanterie-Regiment 324 attacked to relieve pressure on Infanterie-Regiment 307, but both units withdrew by the morning of 14 October. That day, the Germans could see the Soviets, reinforced by units of 99th Rifle Corps, preparing an offensive and decided to retire that night. On 15 October, the Soviets would take time to probe the new German position with relatively weak infantry attacks whilst they planned a set-piece battle to begin the following day. The Germans would repeat the same tactic of retiring at night to frustrate these plans. This also made Soviet attempts to envelop the German line harder to achieve; however, Infanterie-Regiment 307 would be outflanked on 17 October, but MG-Bataillon 4 intervened to stabilize the situation. Infanterie-Regiment 307 would be free to retreat to the north shore of Lake Salmijärvi.

The German commander stated that the Soviets would not launch attacks against an unshaken enemy without careful reconnaissance and the orderly assembly of available supporting weapons. There were no energetic pursuits of rear guards to break or rout these units prior to new positions being occupied.

Luostari was attacked by 99 Soviet aircraft; 33 German aircraft (according to Soviet sources) were destroyed on the ground and five in the air. Here, Soviet Pe-2 bombers are flying over typical northern Arctic terrain. (TASS via Getty Images)

The Tarnet Road

Only Tarnet Road offered the Germans any hope of withdrawal. The achievement of the Soviets in moving a large unit with heavy weapons through what was considered impassable terrain was admired, but the Germans realized they would be exhausted from their five-day march. However, 70th Naval Rifle Brigade continued their move north-west. Canvas bags were used as replacement horseshoes but forage was lacking. The brigade commander, Major-General Zhukov, felt he had to advance to seize German supplies; however, instead of advancing eastwards into the rear of 2.Gebirgs-Division, the Soviets advanced north into the tundra to cut off the Tarnet Road. This move was too ambitious.

The Petsamo–Kirkenes (Tarnet) road was 10km further on from the Arctic Ocean Highway. The officer in charge of the reconnaissance team of 70th Naval Rifle Brigade shot up a German truck using the road and seized the rations on board. On 12 October, the brigade hunkered down in a hollow overgrown with bushes close to a lake. There were bare rock faces with countless crevices on the northern and eastern sides that served as good cover. The guns and mortars were not initially with the brigade, as the horses had fallen behind and would not budge; the weapons needed to be manhandled forward.

On 13 October, the 2nd Battalion of 70th Naval Rifle Brigade, commanded by Major Kalinin, was the first to attack the German defences on the Tarnet Road, but those that got into the German trench system were cut off and suffered heavy losses. German aircraft bombed the hollow, but without inflicting any casualties save on the horses that had made it there. German firing positions had to be suppressed first, and this took the entire day. More success was had at night when the Germans could not deter them with aimed fire. The 1st Battalion reached the small settlement of Kivitunturi. Captain Sidirova with 3rd Battalion and the submachine gun company commanded by Senior Lieutenant Astratov were mentioned by Pestanov (1976) for their outstanding fight for Tarnet Road, which the former asserted was captured by dawn on 14 October.

On 14 October, guns and mortars were in place to assist but made no difference as the Germans had prepared a major counter-attack by II./Gebirgsjäger-Regiment 141 with artillery support from Gebirgs-Artillerie-Regiment 118. Pestanov reported (p. 110) that he had never experienced a bombardment as intensive as this. Although he stated that attempts to push them from the road were not successful, he was being disingenuous, as the Germans successfully retreated along the road that day. On 15 October, Pestanov stated that 2nd Battalion was on heights that could dominate the road and could see destroyed German trucks, but by then the Germans had escaped. Some 18,000 soldiers would retreat along this route. However, the cost was high, with 6.Gebirgs-Division losses for October recorded as 18 officers and 451 enlisted killed, 34 officer and 1,232 enlisted wounded, and five officers and 542 enlisted missing.

Retreating to Petsamo

The 6.Gebirgs-Division was in a vulnerable position. Pemsel, the commanding officer, had obtained the order to withdraw. South of the Russian Road, elements of 14th Rifle Division had advanced and were on the hills overlooking the road at kilometre 6. Traffic to the Petsamo bridges, the northern Prinz Eugen Bridge and the more southerly Speer Bridge, was endangered. Oberstleutnant G. Vogl, the operations officer, suggested to Pemsel that Grenadier-Brigade 388 attack the hill whilst II./Gebirgsjäger-Regiment 141 withdrew to Buchbauer Camp with their vehicles north of the hill unseen by the Soviets. The III./Gebirgsjäger-Regiment 143, at the lower reaches of the Titovka, also needed to move back between Buchbauer and the Schwabenweg (Speer Road). Grenadier-Brigade 388 and Grenadier-Brigade 503 were ordered to form a bridgehead around both bridges over the Petsamo River. The plans were approved, and in a night attack Hauptmann Schneeberger with his III./Grenadier-Brigade 388 cleared the way to Buchbauer, and Rüf's III./Gebirgsjäger-Regiment 143 entered the camp at 0400 hrs on 12 October. The II./Grenadier-Brigade 503 was further north retreating from the Srednyi Peninsula, but could not be reached by a patrol that evening.

At 0730 hrs, 12./Gebirgsjäger-Regiment 143 reported Soviet soldiers, probably from 14th Rifle Division, east of Ivananjärvi heading north. At 0750 hrs, the Soviets were in battalion strength and with heavy weapons fought for Hill 205. The line was not complete and the Soviets moved between III./Gebirgsjäger-Regiment 143 and Grenadier-Brigade 503 further north of Oksentinjärvi. A move to stop them at Hill 211 was carried out, and by evening, two enemy battalions were sealed off. Meanwhile, 13.Kompanie held the lower reverse slopes of Hill 205. Rüf reported how the Soviets approached so close together that the Germans thought they had linked their arms; the Germans opened a devastating fire at 100m. Jodl later reported that Soviet losses here were so heavy that 368th Rifle Division had to replace 14th Rifle Division.

Rüf used messengers to pass on orders; for example, he wanted a heavy machine gun to move to a ridge 200m away; the *Pionier-Zug* needed to occupy a rocky outcrop west of Hill 211 and the messenger had to pass through a hail of bullets to inform them. The message got through, but his messenger was hit and died. He had known him for two years, and during that time the messenger was sentenced to prison for hitting an officer, but was sent to the front in the summer of 1944 when the Soviets advanced into Lithuania. He was wounded and volunteered to join 2.Gebirgs-Division when he recovered. Without knowing he was serving a prison sentence, his wish was granted by the authorities.

Rüf's battalion disengaged during the night. They had grenades thrown at them when they approached the positions of Grenadier-Brigade 503 to identify themselves, but the munitions

The German formations deployed in the Arctic had a long road home. Initially, they thought they would head south, but northern Norway was their destination. Some roads, especially those that led to Lake Inari, were built on marshy terrain and, reinforced with timber, had embankments that offered them some stability. The soldiers, though, often had to give their vehicles a helping hand. (Nik Cornish at www.Stavka.org.uk)

Krautler described how the German soldiers had imagined their departure from the Arctic differently. The senselessness of the war was more apparent than ever. They had thought they would have moved out in good order, rather than being thrown out. This distorted the memory of the time spent in the Arctic. What happened last was remembered first. (Nik Cornish at www.Stavka.org.uk)

landed harmlessly 50m away. White flares were then fired and the soldiers managed to identify themselves. At 0400 hrs on 13 October, they arrived at kilometre 3 on the Schwabenweg and found Grenadier-Brigade 503 soldiers sitting around in groups. Rüf asked the Hauptmann in charge of the Grenadier-Brigade 503 battalion what he was doing there. He replied that a marsh was stopping him reaching the bridgehead. Rüf said he had just got his unit through the same terrain. Further up Rüf then encountered another Grenadier-Brigade 503 battalion, and he assumed command of them, as in a few hours he expected the Soviets to attack on the Schwabenweg then along the Russian Road to the bridge. He had them defend the sharp bend in the road as it ascended a hill. Rüf's unit would be to their right. The III./Grenadier-Brigade 503 was next, then II./Gebirgsjäger-Regiment 143 and two battalions of Grenadier-Brigade 388. Rüf was on the Kuobaroaivi. A battery of light field howitzers supported him. The III./Grenadier-Brigade 503 fired mortars at Hill 211.

The radios used by Rüf were not working; only those used by the artillery could be used. When the gun batteries were ordered to break camp, Rüf was dismayed, as the Soviets 2km below were preparing a major attack. The II./Grenadier-Brigade 503 started to fire. Rüf asked the communications officer what was going on, and was told that the Tarnet Road was blocked, and that the artillery was to move to support the counter-attack by II./Gebirgsjäger-Regiment 141 at Isenkiventunturi. The Soviets on Hill 200 (probably 70th Naval Rifle Brigade, but perhaps 72nd Naval Rifle Brigade) had attacked the baggage train of II./Gebirgsjäger-Regiment 141; the commander, Leutnant Uhl, kept his head and organized a defence. Major Glötzer, the battalion commanding officer, then organized a counter-attack, but was soon hit and wounded. Company commanders *Oberleutnante* Pinsher and Schlapp went on the offensive and took the road. They had the support of 2cm Flak guns deployed in the ground role. This is the event that led to Pemsel ordering the immediate return of the artillery to support this battalion.

Rüf, returning from II./Grenadier-Brigade 503, had the order to cross the Prinz Eugen Bridge at 1300 hrs. His report for 14 October described how III./Grenadier-Brigade 503 was withdrawing without communication with his unit at 1200 hrs. Rüf described how the officers of the Luftwaffe field regiment could probably explain the process of firing a weapon, but would be better at experiencing theory rather than practice. Rüf's 13.Kompanie advanced across the southern slope of the Kuobaroaivi into the flank of the enemy. Then at 1300 hrs, Rüf gave the order for a fighting withdrawal. The II./Grenadier-Brigade 503 set off for the Prinz Eugen Bridge and Rüf's flank was uncovered. At kilometre 3, there was heavy fire from the bush to the south of the road. The road went through marshy terrain heavily interspersed with bush. Machine guns and submachine guns were brought up to the front to break a way through. They were by the Petsamo River, but needed to fight up the bank to reach the bridge. Fired at from all sides, a tributary 30m wide had to be crossed. Oberleutnant Koller's 12.Kompanie was tasked with forming a bridgehead and Oberleutnant Maier's 13.Kompanie with making another bridgehead to keep the way open to the bridge. Oberfeldwebel Ropp's company fought through to the bridge and the other two followed by 1600 hrs.

Rüf, along with the rest of the battalion giving supporting fire, was still south of the tributary when the bridge was destroyed. Twenty of his men tried to swim over the tributary whilst being fired at, but none of them succeeded. Before dusk, the Soviets stormed Rüf's position. Only Rüf, playing dead whilst being searched by Soviet troops, escaped. At night he swam over the river, watching Petsamo burn in the distance. Rüf claimed that the explosive charges on the Prinz Eugen Bridge were detonated too early. He also asserted that the Soviets were not within 300m of the structure and the Germans were not practised enough in withdrawal tactics. He wrote that holding off the enemy and fighting to gain time were unfamiliar to German soldiers who in the last two years had experienced static warfare.

Further south at the Speer Bridge, the situation was even more desperate. On 13 October, 10th Guards Rifle Division was told to begin a push on Petsamo with the support of 7th Guards Tank Brigade and 339th Guards Heavy Self-Propelled Artillery Regiment. They were told that the Petsamo–Tarnet road would be intercepted by a brigade from the 127th Light Rifle Corps. On 14 October, 65th Rifle Division, delayed by the German attack on the road junction west of Luostari, was told to advance on Petsamo to help them. Colonel N. Yurenkov's 7th Guards Tank Brigade deployed five tanks to support 10th Guards Rifle Division's advance on the west bank of the Petsamo. Sappers and infantry from 24th Guards Rifle Regiment were loaded onto the tanks and they advanced towards a road intersection. Yurenkov personally led this force to attempt to block the retreat of German troops. The Soviets advanced down the Arctic Ocean Highway to the Speer Bridge to attempt to cut off the German battalions on the other side of the Petsamo River. By 2200 hrs, an intersection had been captured. Lazarev was ordered to guard the bridge (he is probably referring to the Speer Bridge), but a span had already been destroyed deliberately by the tanks to hinder further retreat. The Germans appeared from the east in the night, and elements of 35th Guards Rifle Regiment ambushed them. Schneeberger's III./Grenadier-Brigade 388 stormed across the Speer Bridge in the face of withering fire. Hauptmann Bleckmann's II./Gebirgsjäger-Regiment 143 was also caught on the wrong side of the river. Bleckmann was wounded and his men wanted to carry him, but he shot himself to spare them the trouble; his battalion suffered 100 casualties crossing the Speer Bridge.

The final push on Petsamo could now begin. Guards Major Guili from 24th Guards Regiment was told to put his soldiers on tanks and take them into the town. The 14th Rifle Division was advancing from the south-east. In the early morning of 15 October, Petsamo was captured. The 10th Guards Rifle Division was withdrawn to the second echelon, having suffered the most among the divisions in terms of casualties, because (according to the divisional commander) the attacking formations were too dense. Excessive arrogance in not properly appreciating the enemy's strengths was also a cause.

The coastal flank

With the envelopment by the Light Rifle Corps delayed, attention turned to the coast. At 2330 hrs on 9 October, 30 ships carrying 2,750 men of 63rd Naval Infantry Brigade (under the command of Colonel A. M. Krylov) began landing on the southern shore of Malaya Volokovaya inlet, to the left of German positions on the Srednyi Peninsula, 30km from Cape Krestovyi, deep in the enemy rear. The intention was to move on the flank and rear of the German defences on the Mustatunturi Range.

Captain 1st Rank Klevenskiy, commander of Patrol Cutter Brigade, was commander of the landing-ship detachment. The three assault detachment commanders were subordinated to him. Commander of the first assault detachment was Guards Captain Zyuzin. The following vessels comprised his detachment: small subchasers MO-423, MO-424, MO-428, MO-429, MO-430, MO-431, MO-433 and MO-434, and torpedo boats TKA-214, TKA-215 and TKA-211.

Captain Third Rank Gritsuk commanded the second assault detachment, consisting of the following vessels: large subchasers BO-213, BO-214, BO-215, BO-216, BO-217, BO-218, BO-219, BO-220, BO-221, BO-222 and BO-224.

Commander of the third assault detachment was Captain 2nd Rank Alekseev. The following vessels comprised his detachment: torpedo boats TKA-204, TKA-206, TKA-207, TKA-208, TKA-210, TKA-213, TKA-222 and TKA-240.

Captain-Lieutenant Antonov was named commander of the mobile screen force, consisting of the following vessels: torpedo boats TKA-234, TKA-238, and TKA-246.

The landing-ship detachment commander was located on the specially equipped torpedo boat TKA-241. The first assault detachment commander was on MO-423, the second assault detachment commander on BO-221 and the third assault detachment commander on TKA-240. The landing force commander could listen to radio traffic between the landing-ship commander and the commanders of the three assault detachments.

At Pummanki, the embarkation due to begin at 1830 hrs had only been completed at 2330 hrs, 1hr 10m late, because the force commander gave instructions to his cutter commanders at a meeting when they should have stayed on their vessels. There were no navigational aids at two of the embarkation moorage sites to assist crews in approaching the moorings, and BO-218 damaged its propellers and had to be removed from the landing detachment. Personnel and cargo had to be redistributed to other ships. The first detachment weighed anchor at 2140 hrs; there was a southerly wind force 4–5 with visibility at 1–2 nautical miles. It moved at 12 knots, holding close to shore. Engine exhausts were diverted below the surface to maintain security. At 2209 hrs, searchlights were switched on and illumination rounds started to be fired. The ships reduced speed to 7 knots to reduce the bow wave. On the approach to Cape Volokovaya, German shore-based observers detected them and more rounds were fired. The ships increased speed to 16 knots and laid smoke from on-board dischargers and floats.

A group under the command of Guards Senior Lieutenant Lyakh (MO-429, MO-430, and TKA-211) moved out of column towards their landing site on the western shore of Cape Punaynenniemi. Small subchasers MO-429 and MO-430 immediately began to offload Captain Barchenko-

Soviet attacks from the Srednyi Peninsula, 9–14 October 1944

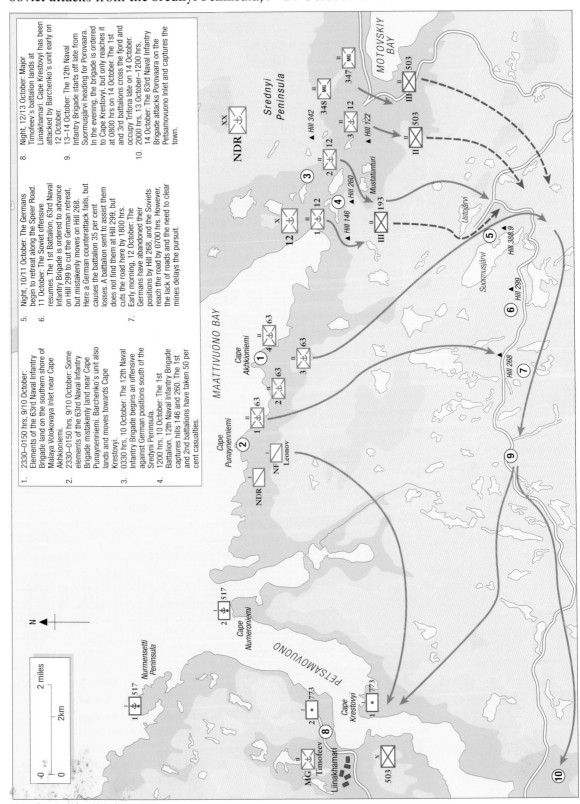

1. 2330–0150 hrs, 9/10 October: Elements of the 63rd Naval Infantry Brigade land on the southern shore of Malaya Volokovaya Inlet near Cape Akhkioniemi.

2. 2330–0150 hrs, 9/10 October: Some elements of the 63rd Naval Infantry Brigade mistakenly land near Cape Punaynenniemi. Barchenko's unit also lands and moves towards Cape Krestovyi.

3. 0330 hrs, 10 October: The 12th Naval Infantry Brigade begins an offensive against German positions south of the Srednyi Peninsula.

4. 1200 hrs, 10 October: The 1st Battalion, 12th Naval Infantry Brigade captures hills 146 and 260. The 1st and 2nd battalions have taken 50 per cent casualties.

5. Night, 10/11 October: The Germans begin to retreat along the Speer Road.

6. 11 October: The Soviet offensive resumes. The 1st Battalion, 63rd Naval Infantry Brigade is ordered to advance on Hill 299 to cut the German retreat, but mistakenly moves on Hill 268. Here a German counterattack fails, but causes the battalion 35 per cent losses. A battalion sent to assist them does not find them at Hill 299, but cuts the road here by 1800 hrs.

7. Early morning, 12 October: The Germans have abandoned their positions by Hill 268, and the Soviets reach the road by 0700 hrs. However, the lack of roads and the need to clear mines delays the pursuit.

8. Night, 12/13 October: Major Timofeev's battalion lands at Liinakhamari. Cape Krestovyi has been attacked by Barchenko's unit early on 12 October.

9. 13–14 October: The 12th Naval Infantry Brigade starts off late from Suormusjärvi heading for Porovaara. In the evening, the brigade is ordered to Cape Krestovyi, but only reaches it at 0800 hrs on 14 October. The 1st and 3rd battalions cross the fjord and occupy Trifona late on 14 October.

10. 2000 hrs, 13 October–1200 hrs, 14 October: The 63rd Naval Infantry Brigade attacks Porovaara on the Petsamovuono Inlet and captures the town.

Emelianov's composite reconnaissance detachment. *TKA-211* attempted to approach the shore three times, but was unable to extend its gangplank and land its small force. Only after landing his troops from *MO-429* did Lyakh, learning of the problem with *TKA-211*, order the torpedo boat by megaphone to go alongside his *MO-429*; the soldiers from *TKA-211* then disembarked across his boat. The vessels of this group completed their landings by 2316 hrs, and, moving away from shore at full speed north-north-west, laid down a smoke screen to cover the other landings occurring at that moment in the area of Cape Akhkioniemi.

Approaching the shore at 2315 hrs, small subchasers *MO-423*, *MO-424*, *MO-428*, *MO-431*, *MO-433*, *MO-434* and torpedo cutters *TKA-214* and *TKA-215* landed their troops in the area of Cape Akhkioniemi. The landings were completed in 15 minutes; there was insignificant enemy artillery and mortar fire. Upon completion of the landing, the cutters withdrew to the north of Cape Akhkioniemi to cover the approach and landing of the second and third waves of the amphibious force. During their withdrawal, the cutters laid down a smoke screen with their on-board dischargers.

The second landing detachment began to approach Cape Akhkioniemi at 2330 hrs, even before the first wave completed its landings. It had departed Pummanki at 2235 hrs, and was detected by enemy searchlights and fired at by shore batteries in the area of Cape Volokovaya at 2315 hrs. Manoeuvring at full speed in a zigzag, the detachment reached the set of green navigational marker lights in Maattivuono Bay and turned towards the landing zone, but because the large subchasers had a draft of 2.14m, they had to go inshore on several occasions and even land their soldiers on a smaller vessel closer to the shore. An insufficient knowledge of the region on the part of the commanders of some of the vessels led to five large subchasers (*BO-219*, *BO-215*, *BO-216*, *BO-222* and *BO-224*) approaching the coastline west of the designated landing site and depositing their troops (elements of 1st Rifle Battalion, the NCO Academy, 3rd Company of 2nd Rifle Battalion, 2nd Company of 4th Rifle Battalion and the brigade medical company) near Cape Punaynenniemi, and not near Cape Akhkioniemi. The pathfinder teams had turned on their markers one after the other as the cutters proceeded past them, and this should have fully supported the orientation of the landing-ship detachments. A pathfinder team went ashore with the first wave, and after seven minutes determined its location and turned on its marking lights. By 0050 hrs on 10 October, the second wave had landed, and its landing vessels began the withdrawal to base at Pummanki.

The smoke screens that were laid down in Maattivuono Bay during the assault by the first and second waves considerably hindered the manoeuvrability of the third wave. The third wave cast off their moorings in Pummanki at 2212 hrs, and proceeded to the landing site at 12 knots. In the transit, the cutters of this wave were illuminated by enemy searchlights and illumination rounds and, just like the first two waves, were fired upon by

The difficulties of landing naval infantry on a rocky shore sometimes were too much for larger boats. Leonov's men had to use gangplanks to access the shore line, but these were not long enough and the crew had to enter the water and keep them above their heads whilst the scouts walked on them. (TASS via Getty Images)

artillery. By 2316 hrs, the third wave had overtaken the second and had to stop for seven minutes, but then landed soon after.

The 3rd and 4th battalions, along with the brigade headquarters, moved inland, and by 0500 hrs on 10 October had reached Hill 124. Brigade staff did not have communications with 1st Battalion and other brigade subunits that had landed in Punaynenniemi Bay. Captain A. Panev, the temporary commander of 1st Battalion, led his men south and then, without support, decided to return to the beach. The 2nd Company under Senior Lieutenant N. Z. Shepetukha maintained radio contact with brigade, who ordered them to move on Hill 299 to prevent the enemy using the road from Titovka to Porovaara. Hill 141 was reached by 0400 hrs on 10 October. Captain S. F. Belousev and part of the 2nd Battalion remained on the beach to search for missing units. The 3rd Battalion commander, Major Krasil'nikova, linked up with 12th Naval Infantry Brigade units in the area of Lake Tiejärvi by 1200 hrs on 10 October.

Also that morning, at 0330 hrs, a 90-minute artillery bombardment by 209 guns firing 47,000 rounds preceded an attack by 12th Naval Infantry Brigade under Colonel V. V. Rassokhin on the Srednyi Isthmus. The previous day had seen German artillery positions targeted. The bombardment on the morning of the attack continued to target them, and guns using direct fire set about destroying bunkers. Smoke and high-explosive rounds were fired at observation posts. The Germans were not able to provide effective artillery support to their front line. Fire from artillery units supporting the naval infantry was adjusted by forward observers as the attack developed. At 0320 hrs, engineer troops and naval infantry groups detonated demolitions and line charges in the enemy barbed-wire obstacles, resulting in the creation of a 1km-long passage lane. The 2nd and 3rd battalions of 12th Naval Infantry Brigade, along with 614th Separate Punishment Company, advanced slowly under heavy machine-gun fire on their designated axes. A snowstorm hindered 1st Battalion on its way to Hill 146, as snow drifts covered the signs engineers had placed to show gaps in the minefield and barbed wire was not removed; however, the weather also disguised their approach.

Kislyakov commanded a submachine-gun company that belonged to Major A. Petrov's 1st Battalion. The initial attack was repulsed, and Petrov ordered Kislyakov to send Lieutenant Sokolov's machine-gun platoon to bypass an enemy height. Senior Sergeant P. Kuydrayov had to jump to grab an enemy machine gun from the hands of a soldier behind a high boulder. Sokolov succeeded in infiltrating behind the enemy position, and hearing his platoon engage the defenders from behind, the rest of the company advanced to the front. The same tactic was repeated against the next height. By 0930 hrs, Major A. Petrov's battalion had seized Hill 146. One battalion in the second echelon under Major A. Paul was committed to capture Hill 260. Anti-tank guns were brought forward to fire into the bunker embrasures. By 1200 hrs, the two battalions had penetrated enemy defences between hills 146 and 260 and broken through to Lake Tiajärvi and the 3rd Battalion of 63rd Naval Infantry Brigade. Losses were heavy, with 1st and 2nd battalions losing 50 per cent of their strength. No further advance was made.

That night, the German retreat started along the Speer Road. At 0800 hrs the following morning, the Soviets noted that the Germans had laid down a smoke screen in the areas of hills 122 and 388.9, apparently to cover their withdrawal. The Germans had abandoned their positions on

Each of the patrol boats could carry about a platoon's worth of infantry. Landings were practised extensively, but the complications co-ordinating so many boats proved too much, and many landed at locations where they were not supposed to. (Sovfoto/UIG via Getty Images)

the isthmus during the night. At 0630 hrs on 11 October, the Soviets continued their offensive and reached the area of hills 270 and 194.7. Units began to move forward to their designated objectives, meeting no enemy resistance. Contact with the enemy was lost. The guns had to be dragged by hand. This demanded a great deal of time and energy. Artillery fell behind, and was able to catch up with the infantry only when it reached the road leading from Mustatunturi to Hill 388.9. The 347th and 348th Separate Machine Gun battalions went into the attack. By 2200 hrs, the 348th had reached the southern slopes of Yaukhonokantunturi hill, and the 347th Hill 109.

By 1000 hrs on 11 October, the 3rd and 4th battalions of 63rd Naval Infantry Brigade reached the area of Hill 388.9. Pursuing the retreating enemy, they reached the southern slopes of hills 388.9 and 326.5 by 1400 hrs. Here, they cut the single road along which the Germans were conducting their withdrawal. The 2nd Battalion, comprising the brigade commander's reserve, was moving up to the area of Lake Ustojärvi at this time. The 1st Battalion fought with enemy forces of upto battalion strength in the area of Hill 268, 1km north of the Titovka–Porovaara Road. Because of mistaken orientation, however, the battalion commander believed he was located near Hill 299. The enemy counter-attacked three times near Hill 268, but each time was driven off. By 1800 hrs, upto 35 per cent of the men were out of action, and the battalion commander went over to the defence on the southern slopes of Hill 268. At the same time, he requested aid from the brigade commander. The 4th Battalion, sent by the brigade commander from Hill 388.9 to Hill 299 to support 1st Battalion, could not find the battalion in that location, because it actually was not there, but near Hill 268. By late evening, 1st Battalion, along with 3rd Company of 2nd Battalion and 2nd Company of 4th Battalion, was in the area of Hill 268; the 2nd and 3rd battalions were in the area of Hill 388.9; and 4th Battalion was in the area of Hill 299. The 1st, 2nd and

3rd battalions of 12th Naval Infantry Brigade were located east of Lake Ustojärvi, and 4th Battalion was on the move from Ozerko to the area of Hill 388.9. Their objective, to cut the road, was achieved a day earlier than expected because of the light resistance offered, but only 6km were gained in two days.

The need to pursue the enemy more energetically after breaking through his defensive positions was attested to by reports from aerial reconnaissance. A sortie flown from Pummanki Airfield at dawn on 10 October observed, for example, the enemy's southward withdrawal from the isthmus. The same pilot observed heavy westward vehicle and cart traffic along the Titovka–Porovaara Road. Separate groups of retreating enemy infantry units were also observed. Fleet Air Forces carried out continuous observation behind the front line and on roads leading out of the battle area in order to stay informed of the situation. It was clear to the Soviets that the Germans were withdrawing ahead of Northern Defensive Region units, covering their retreat with rear-guard units in positions prepared earlier. By this time, Dubovtsev was aware of the enemy's retreat along the entire sector of the Litsa Line. Liaison officers periodically transmitted operational information about the situation in 14th Army's sector to fleet headquarters. By dawn on 12 October, it was clear that the Germans had abandoned their positions on Hill 268. A pursuit was ordered. The 1st Battalion reached the road to Porovaara at 0700 hrs. By 1000 hrs, the entire brigade was on the march, with the reconnaissance company out in front and 2nd Battalion acting as rear-guard. The enemy did not offer any resistance, and the brigade, clearing the road of mines and explosive demolitions, reached the 1940 international border by 1830 hrs. The 12th Naval Infantry Brigade took up defensive positions south-west and south of Lake Ustojärvi to prevent the Germans from evacuating Titovka.

Air reconnaissance on 12 October again observed the retreat of units and movement of German vehicle columns from Petsamo, indicating the Germans were apparently not planning to hold in the Petsamo area. This information could have generated a decision by Dubovtsev to move more quickly to the shore of Petsamovuono Inlet. Changes in the situation in connection with Golokov's decision to capture Liinakhamari port on the night of 12/13 October, and also the rapidly changing situation of the reconnaissance detachments on Cape Krestovyi, also should have prompted his thinking. Only at 0530 hrs on 13 October, after spending the night at the 1940 international border, did 63rd Naval Infantry Brigade set out for Porovaara to assemble on Cape Krestovyi by the end of the day, and to cross over to Liinakhamari in order to seize Trifona upon the arrival of boats. The 12th Naval Infantry Brigade set out from the area of the road intersection between Lakes Ustojärvi and Suormusjärvi at 0850 hrs on 13 October, for movement to Porovaara.

Delays were caused by mine clearing on the road, bridge construction, obstacle removal and the initial absence of supporting artillery that was unable to employ their designated march routes because the single road across Mustatunturi toward Hill 388.9 was mined. The artillery was forced to bypass through Kutovaya and Titovka, a road used by other units. Only on 14 October did the artillery reach the infantry. On 13 October, the infantry was forced to assault Mikulantunturi, where the Germans had established

The naval infantry cleared the wire, but minefields would prove more difficult, as the signs the engineers had laid would be covered with snow. (Sovfoto/UIG via Getty Images)

positions to guard the approach to Porovaara with air support. The brigade reached the outskirts of Porovaara by 2000 hrs, with 4th Battalion on the right flank, 3rd Battalion on the left, 2nd Battalion in the centre and 1st Battalion in reserve. Dubovtsev ordered 12th Naval Infantry Brigade to turn off the Porovaara road on the evening of 13 October and move to Cape Krestovyi. They were to assemble there by 0100 hrs on 14 October for loading on cutters and transit across the bay to Liinakhamari, to assist in the capture of Trifona. The cross-country movement during darkness was so difficult that brigade units lost contact with each other. They had to halt in order to re-establish command and control and reconnoitre the route. As a result of this, the brigade did not arrive at Cape Krestovyi at the designated time, but only by 0800 hrs on 14 October. By this time, Barchenko-Emelianov's reconnaissance detachments had already crossed over to Liinakhamari. The 1st and 3rd battalions of 12th Naval Infantry Brigade occupied Trifona without a fight by late in the evening of 14 October.

The attack on Porovaara was renewed in the early hours of 14 October. The 2nd and 4th battalions captured the town by 1200 hrs. The Germans withdrew to Isomukka and, together with the group from Kuobaroaivi, offered resistance to the brigade's 3rd Battalion. Brigade units approaching Porovaara on the shoreline of Petsamovuono Inlet came under artillery fire. With the arrival of the artillery and the Northern Defensive Region tank company, the Germans started to withdraw to Petsamo. Two small boats transported brigade units, minus artillery, supply trains and 2nd Battalion, across Petsamovuono Inlet to the Trifona settlement area from 0500 to 1000 hrs on 15 October.

Cape Krestovyi and Liinakhamari

Liinakhamari was the main supply loading point for the German forces in theatre. Warehouses were built to stock supplies. Petsamofjord and Liinakhamari were protected by four batteries, and in Liinakhamari Bay there were bunkers for machine guns along the shore as well as barbed wire. The entrance to the bay was guarded by four German 150mm guns on the northern shore of Cape Krestovyi and two 210mm guns on Cape Devkin, on the northern shore of Liinakhamari Bay. At the head of the fjord stood four 150mm guns on Cape Numeroniemi and four 150mm guns on Nurmensetti Peninsula.

A composite force of sailors and naval infantrymen was assembled to capture Cape Krestovyi, comprising the reconnaissance detachment of the Northern Defensive Region, commanded by Captain I. P. Barchenko-Emelianov, and the reconnaissance detachment of Headquarters, Northern Fleet, commanded by Senior Lieutenant Viktor N. Leonov. Barchenko-Emelianov was an experienced naval infantryman, who had served in reconnaissance units of the 12th Naval Infantry Brigade since November

1941. In June 1943, he took command of the Northern Defensive Region reconnaissance detachment, a group of naval infantrymen who had carried out many reconnaissance and raid actions.

Barchenko-Emelianov, as overall commander of the raiding force, received his objective on 11 September, when Leonov and his men joined the composite unit. Other attachments included a team of artillerymen, a group of combat engineers and an unspecified number of medics and radio operators. Total strength was 195 men. For four weeks, the unit rehearsed on terrain on the Rybachi Peninsula similar to Cape Krestovyi. Final preparations included coordination with naval aviation, with Barchenko-Emelianov twice meeting pilots at Pummanki; his brother was a pilot who had been shot down and killed earlier in the war. His men would have 'to cross 30km of enemy territory from the landing site. It lay across marshy swamp and tundra, across hills and almost vertical cliffs. We were ordered to traverse this route, take the jaegers' strongpoint on Cape Krestovyi by storm, capture the batteries, and destroy the enemy garrison if it refused to surrender' (Leonov 1993, pp. 104–05). Admiral Golovko described how the distance needed to be covered in two days through 'hillocks, roadless granite and marshy terrain' (Golovko 1965, p. 213).

At 0100 hrs on 10 October, as described earlier, three ships had broken off from the larger fleet; once the shore was reached, long gangplanks were thrown out, but they were not long enough and the cutter crewmen jumped down and picked up the end. Leonov described how, 'Standing up to their waists in the freezing water, they provided us a dry path to the shore' (Leonov 1993, p. 108). The men landed safely with no casualties. They reported in to fleet headquarters and in a snowstorm began their march south-west. The two groups marched separately in order to be less observable. Makar Babikov, one of Leonov's platoon commanders, described how the camouflage suits iced up and bristled and crackled. They heard a thunderstorm behind them, the opening bombardment on the isthmus.

The valleys were filled with snow, and the man in front, with rope attached, had to check for crevasses. Falling snow covered their tracks. The men sought cover amongst the rocks during the day, and to blend in removed their white camouflage smocks. German reconnaissance aircraft flew low to search the rivers and gullies in vain. By the following morning, 11 October, they had covered 15km in 18 hours and were hidden in bushes at the southern end of Lake Syasijärvi. Barchenko-Emelianov reported how his men 'were overloaded – each carried a five-day supply of food, an enhanced set of ammunition, especially grenades, weapons, explosives, the weight was no less than 40kg. And in the way steep cliffs, marshes, in all 30km from the landing site to the isthmus of Cape Cross in a straight line. And when you consider bypassing all obstacles two if not three times more' (quoted in Kabanov 1977, p. 310). They had rested during the day, but then Leonov received a message from Golokov to get a

Liinakhamari needed to be seized quickly, 'to prevent the Nazis from destroying the quays, warehouses and other installations' (Golovko 1965, p. 214). The assault force was to seize Cape Devkin, capture the port, the military post and the commanding hills in the vicinity of the port, and hold them until reinforcements arrived. Here, the bay and port are shown. (Fastboy via Wikimedia Commons, CC BY-SA 3.0)

ASSAULT ON THE 88MM BATTERY ON CAPE KRESTOVYI (PP. 60–61)

The 88mm battery on Cape Krestovyi dominated the approach to Liinakhamari's dock area. Before Leonov could reach the 88mm battery, he decided to capture a hill that stood to the east of it, located on the eastern side of the cape. Here the Germans had a barracks (**1**) and two machine-gun positions (**2**, **3**) on small hillocks behind a barbed-wire obstruction.

Leonov's men were 20m from the barbed wire (which was laid 40–50m from the high ground) when a rocket went up and hung in the air (**4**). The Germans may have realized they were under attack; according to Babikov, the sentry detecting movement had asked for a password, and might have launched their own illuminations. Perhaps a scout touched the barbed wire, as Leonov reported: 'One small bell jingled, and from various places others responded. The sound travelled around, and a series of coloured flares arched up into the sky … On the other side of the wire a barrack … could be seen' (Leonov 1993, p. 111). Babikov described how the rocket bursts lit up the earthen outlines of the barracks, faced with rocks and grass. Some of Leonov's men threw their jackets, rucksacks, and shelter halves onto the barbed wire (**5**) to help them to cross over, whilst tracer bullets sought them out.

The scout Lysenko (**6**) is shown lifting an iron stanchion that keeps a section of wire in place, calling to his comrades to go under the wire. Another scout is crawling under the wire (**7**); he is armed with a PPSh-41. Commissar Guznenko (**8**) and two other men are already on the other side of the wire. Lysenko would soon be seen by the Germans; wounded by machine-gun fire, he managed to keep the stanchion above the ground by resting on one knee.

move on, as the 12th Naval Infantry Brigade's attack was succeeding.

Barchenko-Emelianov had to march during daylight and wrote how a grenade carried by Private Panteleev exploded, but there were no Germans nearby to hear the noise. By nightfall, they had reached a spur on Petsamo Bay, from which they could view Cape Krestovyi – 'a rocky, black cape hanging over the sea' with 'guns in a high location' (Leonov 1993, p. 111). They descended the vertical cliff in 6 hours using ropes. They then had to climb up another ridge. Once there, beyond the cape they could see Liinakhamari across the bay, alight because of air raids. Dawn was fast approaching. They descended a gentler slope to reach their attack positions. Leonov summoned A. Barinov and A. Nikandrov, his platoon commanders, their deputies, his commissar Guznenkov and the support section chief, and under a poncho used his map to describe his plan. Leonov's 95 men with the artillerymen would assault the four 8.8cm guns sited on a gentle slope on the southern part of the cape. First, they would capture high ground 300m north, to the east of the battery. Barchenko-Emelianov ordered two of his platoons (lieutenants Anatolya Kurbatov and Yuriya Pivovarov) to follow this route, as the high ground in the centre of the cape guarded the landward approaches to the four 150mm coastal guns sited on the water's edge on the northernmost shore of the cape. His remaining platoon (under Lieutenant Alexsandr Petrov) with some engineers with demolitions would then storm the battery along the shore. The signal to start the initial two attacks would be a rocket.

Once on top of the hill, and having captured the barracks, Leonov's men descended 300m to attack the 8.8cm battery. The scouts reached the other side of the elevation and could see below them on a large level platform the four guns, in circular gun positions made from boulders. Two of the guns were already lowering their muzzles towards the slope the scouts were beginning to descend, and soon fired over open sights without properly aiming; shrapnel burst amongst the scouts, forcing them to disperse and seek to approach from the flank. They reached the communication trenches and found cover here. Firing bursts from their submachine guns, and using grenades against the gun pits, they made good progress. Petty Officer 1st Class S. M. Agafonov and Senior Sailor A. P. Pshenichnykh clambered on top of a dugout near a gun and ambushed the crew as they exited. Most of the Germans had fled. The guns were captured intact with range finders working, but Barinov was killed, as was Lysenko.

Barchenko-Emelianov's men soon captured the strongpoint closest to the 15cm battery, having to cross barbed wire. German survivors from both attacks made a disorganized withdrawal to the now alerted 15cm battery. Barchenko-Emelianov established his deputy Sintsov with a radio in a captured enemy strongpoint. Kurbatov and Pivovarov with their platoons pressed on to the gun battery. Senior sailors A. Rozaev and A. Sidorov disabled one of the guns with grenades. Rozaev was hit and Sidorov tried to save him, but both were killed by a grenade. Well dug-in Germans in bunkers

If the landing at Liinakhamari was to succeed, the guns on Cape Krestovyi had to be neutralized. Golovko wrote how 'Its success might greatly assist the passage of our warships into the interior of Petsamovuono [Petsamofjord] and accelerate the capture of Pechenga [Petsamo]' (1965, pp. 212–13). There were also two 210mm guns on Cape Devkin, on the northern shore of Liinakhamari Bay. Shown here immediately in front is Cape Devkin; Cape Krestovyi is on the other side of the approach into Liinakhamari Bay. (Fastboy via Wikimedia Commons, CC BY-SA 3.0)

and trenches behind barbed wire repulsed the assault on the other guns. Petrov, sent around the east flank to attack along the shore, was driven back by the rising tide. Barchenko-Emelianov reported to headquarters that he was unable to capture or destroy the guns. The German gun crews, however, suppressed by the scouts' fire from the dominating terrain, were unable to man the remaining guns and would not fire their guns during the fight.

Leonov's men, having captured the 8.8cm gun position, were fired at by German batteries from around the bay, including Cape Devkin, and this caused serious casualties; he 'ordered the men to remove the breech blocks from the cannons and crawl towards the nearest ridge, from which we could over watch the destroyed battery' (Leonov 1993, p. 113). Two enemy cutters were seen in the bay, and Leonov sent two sections to the shore to repel the landing. More ships were seen, and landed about two platoons to the south, in order that they would approach the cape from below the height the scouts previously had to traverse. One group surprised Leonov, and he ran to engage them in close combat. Rifle butts were used as the Germans, up against a cliff edge they had climbed, had nowhere to go. Soviet aircraft also offered their support. According to Golovko, his pilots made ten airstrikes and dropped several parachute containers of ammunition and provisions. The Il-2 Shturmoviks received target designations by signal flares. Soviet ground artillery from the Srednyi Peninsula also helped.

At midday, Leonov asked Barchenko-Emelianov for reinforcements and was given Petrov's platoon plus two sections from Pivovarov's platoon. With these reinforcements, by dusk Leonov had retaken the battery position and adjacent shore. Babikov described the scouts taking 90 prisoners. By nightfall, the area was quiet, except for an occasional outburst of gunfire. The following morning, they would fire at Liinakhamari, setting a gasoline tank and a wooden warehouse ablaze.

By 2000 hrs on 12 October, Barchenko-Emelianov was informed by radio that Liinakhamari harbour would be assaulted in three hours. They observed how the landing force was fired upon by several German shore batteries, but the guns on Cape Krestovyi did not engage them, either because they were destroyed or the crews were preoccupied by the scouts. Barchenko-Emelianov wrote how, early on the morning of 13 October, before daylight, they made several additional attempts to penetrate into the area of the 150mm battery, but the steep slopes and dense fire of defensive fortifications that covered the approaches prevented them from accomplishing their task. Golovko then ordered Leonov with two platoons to cross into the port.

Later in the day, Barchenko-Emelianov on Cape Krestovyi sent Senior Sailor A. Kashtanov, a German speaker with Leonov's unit, to the battery along with a captured officer from the 8.8cm battery, to

The approach of the motor boats into the bay was a fraught affair. However, smoke screens hampered the ability of German batteries at the entrance to Petsamofjord to target them. Here, motor boats are taking Soviet naval infantry across the bay. (Sovfoto/UIG via Getty Images)

persuade them to surrender. When they approached, they were fired upon and the German officer pressed himself into the granite in fright. They gave the officer a white flag, and this was enough to stop the fire. The officer went into the battery position and 30 minutes later emerged with the garrison. By 1800 hrs, Kashtanov had helped register 78 names of German prisoners of war. When the battery position was searched, a drunken German officer was found; they were unable to rouse him. By then, Liinakhamari was secure. In three days of battle for Krestovyi and Liinakhamari, the raiding force lost 53 men killed and wounded, or 27 per cent of their 195-man force. Barchenko-Emelianov, Leonov and two enlisted men were awarded the gold star and title of Hero of the Soviet Union.

The support provided by Il-2 Shturmovik aircraft to the scouts on Cape Krestovyi helped defeat the German counter-attack. Armed with bombs, rockets and 23mm guns, the aircraft was a potent close air support asset that could fly low and fast and was difficult to hit. (Sovfoto/UIG via Getty Images)

The assault on Liinakhamari

A total of 660 men ('volunteers from ships and fleet units and from machine-gun battalions on Rybachi' – Golovko 1965, p. 214) participated in the assault under the command of Major I. A. Timofeev, who was the commander of the 349th Separate Machine-gun Battalion. Colonel Borovikov (the commander of the 125th Naval Infantry Regiment) hastily assembled 320 men – some from an NCO school, others from a naval infantry scout company and the rest from ships' crews based at Poliarnyi – because the staff had not allocated sufficient landing forces at the planning stage. The commander of the naval infantry was Senior Lieutenant B. F. Peterburgsky. A squadron of torpedo boats supported the assault landing. The leading boat in each group was guided by a pilot familiar with the bay.

At 2040 hrs on 12 October, Captain-Lieutenant A. O. Shabalin (subsequently a rear admiral, and twice-awarded Hero of the Soviet Union), with two D-3 torpedo boats (*TKA-116* and *114*) commanded by Lieutenant Litovchenko and Captain-Lieutenant E. A. Uspensky, departed Pummanki with the first wave of the assault force on board. Shabalin on Litovchenko's boat knew the harbour. They had torpedoes, despite the wishes of Petersburgsky (he had wanted the boats to carry more soldiers), to breach the anti-submarine boom and nets. Carrying 52 sailors of the landing force, 'mainly volunteer petty officers and ratings from the MTB and submarine flotillas' (Golovko 1965, p. 215), the men armed with submachine guns were organized in two platoons commanded by Petersburgsky and Lieutenant Alexandrov. Golokov described how the 'landing of parties directly onto harbour quays whose approaches were raked by fire was a difficult business' (1965, p. 214). Each boat was assigned a quay to land at. If they could not land at their quay, they were told to land at the closest beach. The first and second groups were armed with 18 light machine guns, 193 submachine guns, 80 rifles and four to eight hand grenades per naval infantryman, plus

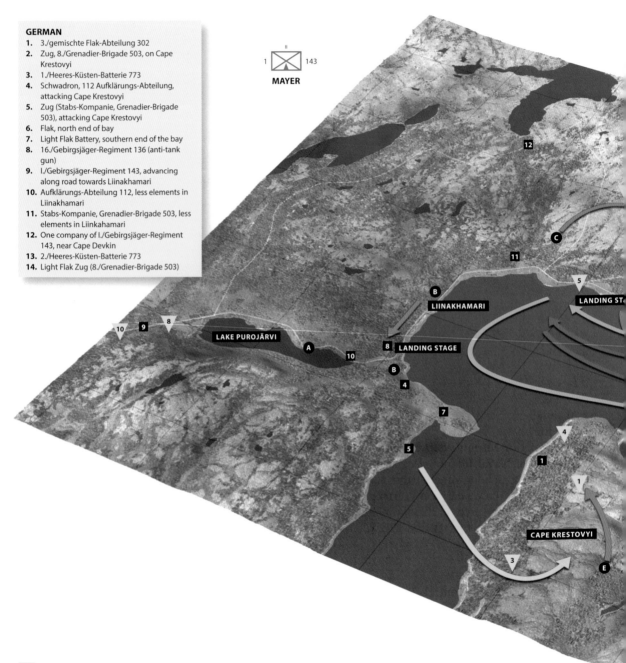

GERMAN

1. 3./gemischte Flak-Abteilung 302
2. Zug, 8./Grenadier-Brigade 503, on Cape Krestovyi
3. 1./Heeres-Küsten-Batterie 773
4. Schwadron, 112 Aufklärungs-Abteilung, attacking Cape Krestovyi
5. Zug (Stabs-Kompanie, Grenadier-Brigade 503), attacking Cape Krestovyi
6. Flak, north end of bay
7. Light Flak Battery, southern end of the bay
8. 16./Gebirgsjäger-Regiment 136 (anti-tank gun)
9. I./Gebirgsjäger-Regiment 143, advancing along road towards Liinakhamari
10. Aufklärungs-Abteilung 112, less elements in Liinakhamari
11. Stabs-Kompanie, Grenadier-Brigade 503, less elements in Liinakhamari
12. One company of I./Gebirgsjäger-Regiment 143, near Cape Devkin
13. 2./Heeres-Küsten-Batterie 773
14. Light Flak Zug (8./Grenadier-Brigade 503)

MAYER

LANDING STAGE

LIINAKHAMARI

LAKE PUROJÄRVI

CAPE KRESTOVYI

▼ EVENTS

1. Early morning, 12 October: Senior Lieutenant Leonov's Northern Fleet scouts attack and overrun 3./gemischte Flak-Abteilung 302 on Cape Krestovyi.

2. Early morning, 12 October: Captain Barchenko-Emelianov's Northern Defensive Region naval scouts attack the positions of 1./Heeres-Küsten-Batterie 773, but fail to capture the battery.

3. Morning, 12 October: Elements of the Stabs-Kompanie of Grenadier-Brigade 503 and Aufklärungs-Abteilung 112 land on Cape Krestovyi, and Leonov retreats from the Flak battery. The Germans push on to the strongpoint situated between the Heeres-Küsten-Batterie and Flak batteries, but the Soviet defences, supported by fighter-bombers, hold.

4. Early evening, 12 October: Leonov, supported by one platoon and two squads from the Northern Defensive Region scouts, retakes the Flak battery and shore.

5. 2302–2330 hrs, 12 October: Major Timofeev's composite battalion lands at Liinakhamari. The first two boats land at landing stages 4 and 5, and the second wave

of five torpedo boats lands between landing stages 2 and 5. Of the third wave of seven boats, two fail to reach the bay.

6. 0200 hrs, 13 October: 2./Heeres-Küsten-Batterie 773 on Cape Devkin is captured by the 4th Machine-Gun Company.

7. Morning, 13 October: A company of naval infantry reinforces Barchenko-Emelianov. At dawn, the Cape Krestovyi battery surrenders.

8. c. 1130 hrs, 13 October: I./Gebirgsjäger-Regiment 143 approaches from Petsamo and joins up with what remains of the garrison and elements of Aufklärungs-Abteilung 112. Mayer's men reach the quays, but are quickly forced back.

9. 1200 hrs, 13 October: Mayer's unit temporarily recaptures the positions of 2./Heeres-Küsten-Batterie 773.

10. Mid-afternoon, 13 October: I./Gebirgsjäger-Regiment 143 and elements of Aufklärungs-Abteilung 112 are attacked by Soviet aircraft near Lake Purojärvi, and withdraw.

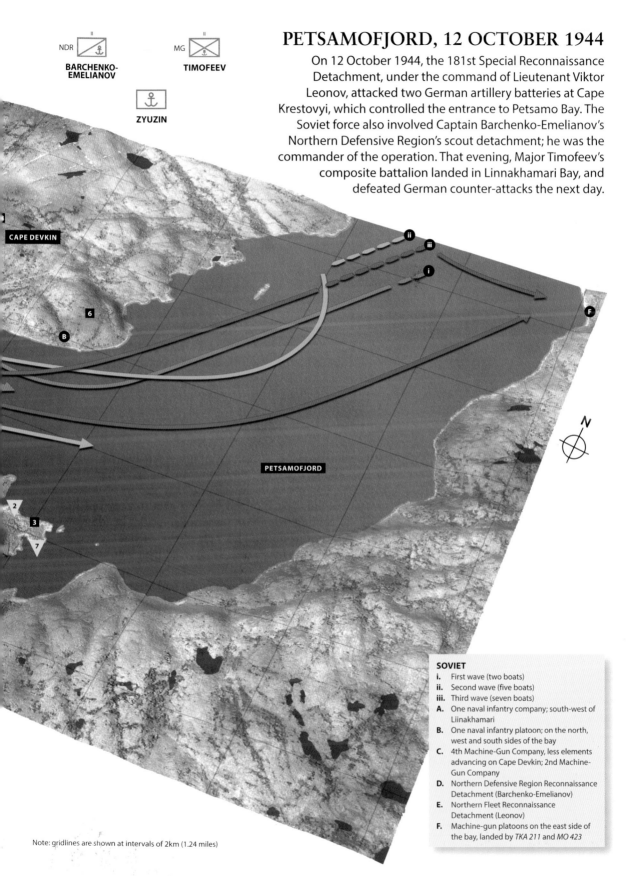

NDR
BARCHENKO-EMELIANOV

MG
TIMOFEEV

ZYUZIN

PETSAMOFJORD, 12 OCTOBER 1944

On 12 October 1944, the 181st Special Reconnaissance Detachment, under the command of Lieutenant Viktor Leonov, attacked two German artillery batteries at Cape Krestovyi, which controlled the entrance to Petsamo Bay. The Soviet force also involved Captain Barchenko-Emelianov's Northern Defensive Region's scout detachment; he was the commander of the operation. That evening, Major Timofeev's composite battalion landed in Linnakhamari Bay, and defeated German counter-attacks the next day.

CAPE DEVKIN

6

B

PETSAMOFJORD

2

3

7

N

Note: gridlines are shown at intervals of 2km (1.24 miles)

SOVIET

i.   First wave (two boats)
ii. Second wave (five boats)
iii. Third wave (seven boats)
A.   One naval infantry company; south-west of Liinakhamari
B.   One naval infantry platoon; on the north, west and south sides of the bay
C.   4th Machine-Gun Company, less elements advancing on Cape Devkin; 2nd Machine-Gun Company
D.   Northern Defensive Region Reconnaissance Detachment (Barchenko-Emelianov)
E.   Northern Fleet Reconnaissance Detachment (Leonov)
F.   Machine-gun platoons on the east side of the bay, landed by *TKA 211* and *MO 423*

1,500 rounds for each machine gun, 600 rounds for each submachine gun and 200 rounds for each rifle.

During the transit towards Petsamovuono Inlet, the two boats were illuminated by a searchlight from Nurmensetti Peninsula, and immediately thereafter fired upon by shore batteries. The cutters fell under artillery and smaller-calibre gunfire from Cape Numeroniemi near the entrance to the inlet. The shells fell short of their targets. Because the Germans were firing high-explosive and illumination rounds, the cutter commanders easily found the entrance to the inlet. Breaking through the fire curtain, they entered the inlet. The cutters proceeded into it, hugging the western shore and, skirting Cape Devkin, at 2250 hrs found moorage No. 5 (the fueling pier) and Liinakhamari Bay. *TKA-116* approached the shore east of moorage No. 5 at 2302 hrs, and landed a 25-man assault force in two minutes. At the same time, the other cutter of this group (*TKA-114*) landed 27 men on the eastern part of moorage No. 4. The cutters came under fire from shore-based artillery, mortars and machine guns on the approach to the landing site and during the landing. After the landing, *TKA-114* remained near the pier to assist the other cutters. Uspensky, with three crew armed with a machine gun, went ashore to occupy nearby barns to secure the immediate vicinity. Only when the second and third waves had landed did Uspensky's boat leave; however, the boat became caught in torpedo nets and lit by a searchlight, was hit repeatedly. The steering gear was inoperable and the boat could only change course through altering the speeds of the two engines. In the meantime, *TKA-116* withdrew towards Cape Devkin, where it met and led first the second and then the third group of cutters toward the docks.

The second group of cutters, commanded by Captain S. G. Koroschunovich, each carrying 70 naval infantrymen but no torpedoes, departed from Pummanki dock at 2047 hrs, moving in column towards Petsamovuono Inlet. This group followed the first group of cutters at a distance of 2,000–3,000m. Just like the leading group, they fell into the beam of a searchlight, shining from Nurmensetti Peninsula. In addition, they were lit up by illumination rounds. This helped the cutters determine the location of the entrance to the inlet, already covered by a smoke screen laid down earlier.

Koroschunovich knew that the first group had been illuminated by searchlights and fired upon by shore batteries. Therefore, he ordered a decrease in speed to 'slow ahead', and when the searchlight beam fell on *TKA-204*, he ordered the laying of a smoke screen towards Nurmensetti. The remaining torpedo boats, moving out of the searchlight's beam, began to break into Petsamovuono Inlet at full speed. They again fell into the beam of a searchlight from Cape Numeroniemi and were fired upon from the same cape. The boats returned suppressive fire at both the battery and the searchlight position, and forced their way into the inlet, hugging the western shore.

During the approach to Cape Devkin, they were illuminated by flares and received concentrated artillery, mortar and machine-gun fire. Under the cover of brief smoke screens that obscured the entire harbour with dense smoke, the cutters almost simultaneously reached their designated landing sites at 2310 hrs. *TKA-204* and *TKA-213* landed their troops on the shore just east of the burning pier No. 5; *TKA-206* and *TKA-207* between piers No. 3 and No. 4; and *TKA-208* 50m from pier No. 2. In spite of heavy

German fire, only *TKA-208* was struck in the left side, and a second round entered the forward cabin from the right side. As a result, the right motor was disabled and three men were killed; however, the motor was quickly repaired and the cutter was able to proceed to the exit from Petsamovuono Inlet. *TKA-204* remained in the landing area to guide the third group at Cape Devkin and then moved towards the exit of the inlet. The smoke screen hanging in the bay was being pushed to the north by the wind, and the cutters were illuminated by a searchlight from Cape Numeroniemi and fired upon by enemy shore batteries during their withdrawal. They had to lay down a new smoke screen and safely returned to Pummanki.

The naval infantry of the first wave experienced heavy small-arms fire when they began to disembark. A petrol tank was hit by an incendiary shell and set alight. This was no accident: a captured German officer later told how they had targeted the petrol tank as they presumed burning oil would rush into the bay and set the boats alight. This did not occur, but the blazing oil did assist the coastal batteries in targeting the boats.

The assault troops began a stubborn battle for the shore. A pier was rigged to explode and G. Ivanov jumped into the water and quickly cut the wires. Petersburgsky was fired at by an artillery bunker with a 75mm gun, but his men advanced and the position was captured. Alexandrov's men jumped into a coal dock. He was wounded, and Senior Sergeant I. P. Katorzhnyi assumed command. He was the first to jump onto the pier and enter into combat. In a short battle, he eliminated enemy positions to enable the second group to land, and they spread out along the beach. The fuel bunkers and pier were captured. An anti-aircraft gun was firing from a two-storey building (the hotel) at the end of the harbour: Petersburgsky's men stormed the building. Together with Private Korolev, Senior Sergeant Katorzhnyi broke into the building and raised a red flag on the roof. Katorzhnyi was awarded the Hero of the Soviet Union title for valour and heroism.

Lieutenant N. Shapovalov's boat (*TKA-208*) from the second group landed his soldiers commanded by Senior Lieutenant Alekseev on the beach 50m from the pier. Alekseev was wounded from fire from a warehouse. Shapovalov ordered his machine gunner to fire at the warehouse. Shapovalov reported that he told Sergeant Katorzhnyi on the shore that he needed to take command; with sailors Popkov and Lukin from *TKA-208*, Katorzhnyi led naval infantrymen to the warehouse whilst the other crewmen unloaded ammunition. When Popkov and Lunkin returned, the boat started its engines and pulled out into the bay. Tracer hit the vessel 100–150m from the smoke screen, and both engines gave out. Lukin and Ridkin were able to start one engine, and the boat reached the protection of the smoke screen. The gasoline tanks were ruptured and the motor stalled again. Despite the difficulties, the boat managed to return to base.

The cutters of the third group commanded by Guard Captain S. D. Zyuvin, carrying Major I. Timofeev's machine-gun troops, proceeded behind the second group towards their landing sites. The distance between these two groups did not exceed 3,000m. Prior to reaching the entrance to Petsamovuono Inlet, the third group set their speed at 8–12 knots. After the second group entered the inlet, Zyuvin increased speed to 18 knots, and at this speed forced his way past the artillery fire from the batteries on Ristiniemi and Numeroniemi. The smoke from the previously laid screen helped the cutters enter the inlet without losses. They moved in dense smoke to the landing

The garrison at Liinakhamari comprised elements of Aufklärungs-Abteilung 112 light 20mm gun batteries, a 7.5cm anti-tank gun and the Stabs-Kompanie of Grenadier-Brigade 503. Here, a German detachment is in a typical stone entrenchment by a fjord. (Keystone-France/Gamma-Keystone via Getty Images)

site, smoke that was particularly thick in the area of Cape Devkin. *TKA-211*, moving at the back of the group, veered off from the forward-moving column, and lost its orientation in the smoke. This cutter landed its 57 troops under the command of Lieutenant Rekalo not on the western, but on the eastern shore of Petsamovuono Inlet, almost opposite Liinakhamari Bay. Under enemy fire, mainly from the area south-west of Liinakhamari Bay, the other boats reached the landing site between the piers; however, *MO-423* could not land its troops at the designated point between docks 3 and 5, because a mortar round had wounded its navigator and two sailors. The helmsman was also wounded, and the starboard motor damaged. The boat landed on the eastern shore of the bay near Cape Krestovyi. *MO-428* ran aground after landing the soldiers near Cape Devkin because the captain sought refuge in the smoke present here. The crew were put on other boats when attempts to refloat *MO-428* failed.

Timofeev launched a swift attack on the eastern and southern slopes of Cape Devkin. By 0200–0300 hrs on 13 October, his group were moving inland under intense light machine-gun, artillery and mortar fire. They reached and captured the battery firing positions. At dawn on 13 October, two companies of German infantry from I./Gebirgsjäger-Regiment 143 sent from Petsamo made their way to the 210mm battery firing positions, counter-attacked and pushed the assault force away from the battery position. The Germans were repulsed by the fire of 1st Machine-Gun Company and several hand-to-hand engagements. By 1200 hrs, the entire battery area was in the hands of the assault force, and the Germans had withdrawn. Then, another two German companies from Trifona attacked Petersburgsky north of Lake Purojärvi. New enemy units were arriving on trucks from Trifona, and assembling near Lake Purojärvi, with the goal of driving the assault force from Liinakhamari. At this same time, during the afternoon, the Germans again moved against the 210mm battery, but all their attacks were beaten off with heavy losses.

Soviet aircraft conducting air reconnaissance observed the approach of German units by road from Trifona settlement to Liinakhamari, and reported this upon their return to the airfield at Pummanki. At about this same time, Timofeev reported enemy troop concentrations in the area of Lake Purojärvi, and requested air support. Despite the approaching darkness (it was nearly 1700 hrs), it was decided to dispatch aircraft. Six Il-8s, six Kittyhawks and four Yaks took off from Pummanki Airfield between 1645 and 1800 hrs. The pilots made four low-level attacks against the designated targets. The fighter cover also participated in the ground attacks. According to the pilots, the marking of their own positions by the assault force units, as well as designation of enemy targets, was executed in a most helpful manner. Timofeev reported to headquarters how 'all the granite hillocks are shrouded in fire and smoke' (quoted in Golovko 1965, p. 216). The Germans suffered heavy losses as a result of the air strikes on forces in the area of Lake Purojärvi, and were not able to withstand the renewed attack of Major Timofeev's composite detachment. The Germans could not hold back the forward surge of the naval infantrymen and, suffering heavy losses, began to withdraw towards Lake Trifonajärvi at 1800 hrs on 13 October.

THE SECOND PHASE, 14–22 OCTOBER 1944

The next stage of the operation was planned as follows: in the north a pursuit into Norway along the Tarnet Road prior to an advance on Kirkenes, in the centre an advance to the Pasvik River in Norway, and in the south an advance down the Nikel Road to capture the Nikel mines. The 131st Rifle Corps (with 45th Rifle Division from Group Pigarevich, 7th Guards Tank Brigade and 275th Special Purpose Motorized Battalion), 99th Rifle Corps (with 73rd Separate Guards Heavy Tank Regiment, 339th Guards Heavy Self-Propelled Artillery Regiment, 284th Special Purpose Motorized Battalion and an engineer battalion with a heavy pontoon bridge) and 31st Rifle Corps (with 89th Separate Tank Regiment and 339th Guards Heavy Self-Propelled Artillery Regiment) were assigned these objectives, respectively.

The 31st Rifle Corps was not committed to combat during the initial phase of the operation and lacked trucks to bring forward supplies. The formation was between 30 and 45km south-east of Luostari on 16 October, and had a long approach march that started that night in the rain. By 18 October, they were on the Luostari–Nikel Road. By midnight, they were expected to be ready to attack towards Nikel, with 367th Rifle Division leading. Lieutenant General Shcherbakov, the commander of 14th Army, had given the unit two artillery regiments, three mortar regiments, two regiments of multiple rocket launchers, a regiment of T-34s, a depleted regiment of 152mm self-propelled guns and three battalions of combat engineers. Divisional and regimental artillery units had only between 25 and 33 per cent of their normal amount of ammunition. The 367th Rifle Division had only 20 per cent of its normal allocation of 82mm and 120mm mortar ammunition. The 122mm gun ammunition was also at 20 per cent, 76mm gun ammunition of the division's artillery regiment was at 25 per cent, 76mm gun ammunition of the regimental batteries was at 30 per cent and 45mm anti-tank gun ammunition was at 40 per cent. The 127th Light Rifle Corps was ordered on a wide flanking move to interdict the Nikel Road south of Nikel in support of 31st Rifle Corps.

The 10th Guards Division was to operate further north and cross into Norway to advance on Kirkenes from the south. The 126th Light Rifle Corps, by attempting a wide enveloping movement south of Kirkenes, was intended to play a vital role in the new offensive, and 86 tons of supplies, most of which were intended for the formation, were brought into Luostari Airfield up to 19 October.

On 15 October, Generaloberst Rendulic met with General der Gebirgstruppe Jodl and ordered 6.Gebirgs-Division to defend the Kirkenes area whilst 2.Gebirgs-Division and 163.Infanterie-Division would defend the Nikel area. Jodl realized the main Soviet attack would be launched at Nikel. The 6.Gebirgs-Division was responsible for the Tarnet Road, Infanterie-Regiment 307 was along the Arctic Ocean Highway, and a battalion of

Infanterie-Regiment 324 supported elements of Gebirgsjäger-Regiment 137 on the Nikel Road. The I. and III./Grenadier-Brigade 193 were also defending positions along the Nikel Road. The German defensive was concentrated on the Nikel axis. Here, 15,000 men would encounter 15,000 Soviets, but the Soviets had the advantage in artillery: they deployed twice the number of guns. Tanks and close air support were also provided. The terrain favoured the defenders. High, rocky hills devoid of vegetation were interspersed with ravines and areas of swamp. Off-road movement for vehicles was not an option. The highest hill, Hill 631, stood at 580m. Streams with steep banks in marshy areas represented difficult obstructions to movement. The road was the only clear path through, and the Germans cratered the surface, laid barricades and planted mines. Defensive positions were sited to prevent the uninterrupted clearing of these obstacles, and could interdict movement.

Festung Nikel had an outer defensive area that comprised six bases laid out within a 5km radius to the south and east of the mines. The bases were 5–8km from each other. There were three battalions of 8.8cm guns and numerous 2cm guns in them, but Rüf and Krautler asserted that their Luftwaffe crews had already spiked most of the heavy guns. On 15 October, Aufklärungs-Abteilung 67 moved into Nikel and took up residence in the abandoned stone-built workers' houses. A high chimney was the most visible feature. The paymaster ordered them to destroy the provisions they found there, in accordance with the scorched-earth order. The reconnaissance battalion was sent to the outer bases on 18 October.

Into Norway

On 18 October, 131st Rifle Corps along the Tarnet Road pushed into Norwegian territory towards Kirkenes. In the north, 4th Battalion, 12th Naval Infantry Brigade landed that day in support of the advance of 45th Rifle Division. At 1350 hrs, 45th Rifle Division moved into Norway. Over the next three days, the division pushed through steep and rocky hills, lakes and swamps to cover 30km along the Tarnet Road. The 14th Rifle Division was then moved to help this division on its left flank; with a tank unit that attempted to negotiate off-road terrain, they wanted to move around the German right flank, however, a swamp 4km from the road prevented the tanks from reaching the road, and they had to retreat and go on the road with 45th Rifle Division. The 1226th Rifle Regiment from 368th Rifle Division succeeded in reaching the naval infantry at Bjørndal. The 45th and 14th Rifle divisions had reached the southern and eastern shores of Jarfjorden. On 23 October, 3rd and 4th battalions, 12th Naval Infantry Brigade and 176 men of the 125th Naval Infantry Regiment under Petersburgsky embarked at Liinakhamari and landed at Kobbholmfjorden in support of the advance on Kirkenes. They captured a hydroelectric power station intact, and cleared the coast to Jarfjorden. The 131st Rifle Corps had advanced 25–30km; opposition was light, with 6.Gebirgs-

On 18 October, 131st Rifle Corps on the Tarnet Road pushed into Norwegian territory towards Kirkenes. In five days, an advance of up to 30km was made. The 6.Gebirgs-Division had fought delaying actions from carefully chosen positions. The 99th Rifle Corps on their southern flank was having a more difficult time. The Norwegian border along the Pasvik River was only reached on 22 October. The river was crossed with amphibious jeeps, and engineers set up a bridge the next day. The 126th Light Rifle Corps, moving on Lake Klistervatn, was less effective than expected due to logistical shortages, and could advance no further than 99th Rifle Corps. (Courtesy of the Central Museum of the Armed Forces, Moscow via Stavka)

Advance on Nikel and Kirkenes

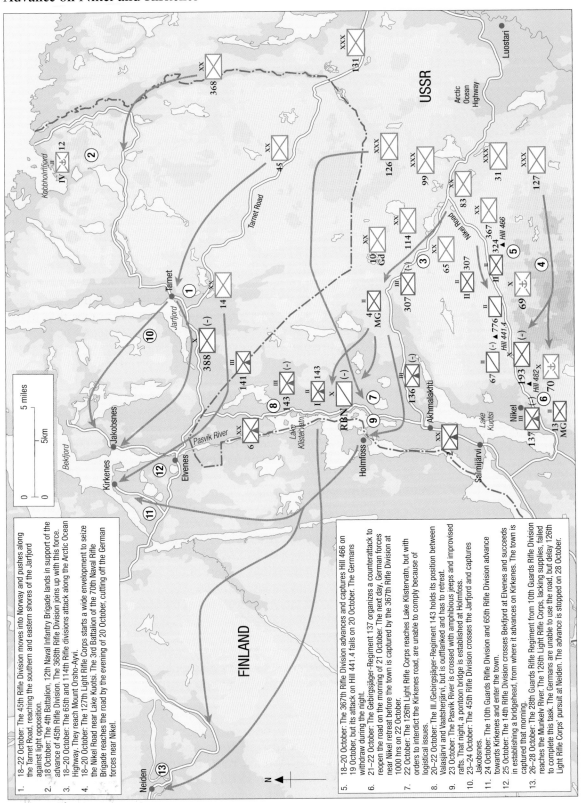

1. 18–22 October: The 45th Rifle Division moves into Norway and pushes along the Tarnet Road, reaching the southern and eastern shores of the Jarfjord against light opposition.

2. 18 October: The 4th Battalion, 12th Naval Infantry Brigade lands in support of the advance of 45th Rifle Division. The 368th Rifle Division joins up with this force.

3. 18–20 October: The 65th and 114th Rifle divisions attack along the Arctic Ocean Highway. They reach Mount Orsho-Ayvi.

4. 18–20 October: The 127th Light Rifle Corps starts a wide envelopment to seize the Nikel Road near Lake Kuotsi. The 3rd Battalion of the 70th Naval Rifle Brigade reaches the road by the evening of 20 October, cutting off the German forces near Nikel.

5. 18–20 October: The 367th Rifle Division advances and captures Hill 466 on 19 October, but its attack on Hill 441.4 fails on 20 October. The Germans withdraw during the night.

6. 21–22 October: The Gebirgsjäger-Regiment 137 organizes a counterattack to reopen the road on the morning of 21 October. The next day, German forces near Nikel retreat before the town is captured by the 367th Rifle Division at 1000 hrs on 22 October.

7. 22 October: The 126th Light Rifle Corps reaches Lake Klistervatn, but with orders to interdict the Kirkenes road, are unable to comply because of logistical issues.

8. 20–22 October: The III./Gebirgsjäger-Regiment 143 holds its position between Valasjärvi and Vaatsherjärvi, but is outflanked and has to retreat.

9. 23 October: The Pasvik River is crossed with amphibious jeeps and improvised rafts. That night, a pontoon bridge is established at Holmfoss.

10. 23–24 October: The 45th Rifle Division crosses the Jarfjord and captures Jakobsnes.

11. 24 October: The 10th Guards Rifle Division and 65th Rifle Division advance towards Kirkenes and enter the town.

12. 25 October: The 14th Rifle Division crosses Bekfjord at Elvenes and succeeds in establishing a bridgehead, from where it advances on Kirkenes. The town is captured that morning.

13. 26–28 October: The 28th Guards Rifle Regiment from 10th Guards Rifle Division reaches the Munkelv River. The 126th Light Rifle Corps, lacking supplies, failed to complete this task. The Germans are unable to use the road, but delay 126th Light Rifle Corps' pursuit at Neiden. The advance is stopped on 28 October.

The rarity of roads made them targets for aircraft, providing the weather permitted them to fly. Wheeled transport was vulnerable to strafing attack, as seen here, but the Germans could use the roads at night, and set demolitions to delay their pursuers. (Courtesy of the Central Museum of the Armed Forces, Moscow via Stavka)

Division fighting rear-guard actions on dominating terrain.

The 99th Rifle Corps was fighting determined resistance on the Arctic Ocean Highway. On 18 October, 114th Rifle Division attacked German positions on Hill 234 frontally and was thrown back, but then an envelopment that night around the position, accompanied by another frontal attack, was successful. Infanterie-Regiment 307 withdrew at night to hills 332.9 and 313, where the 13th Separate Machine-Gun Battalion was located. The Soviets moved artillery forward. After a brief bombardment, the infantry of 114th Rifle Division attacked. By 1800 hrs, they had reached the western slopes. On 20 October, units of 114th and 65th Rifle divisions, advancing 5–7km, by the end of the day had reached the line of the eastern slopes of hills 252, 275.7 and Mount Orsho-Ayvi. Both divisions had moved forward 5–7km. A regiment from 65th Rifle Division cut the road, and the Germans had to abandon their trucks and two artillery pieces and move across the tundra. On 20 October, Il-2 Shturmoviks launched attacks on artillery batteries south-east of Akhmalakhti, destroying two, and stores of ammunition and trucks. Some 452 sorties were flown that day.

On the night of 20 October, Rüf's III./Gebirgsjäger-Regiment 143 was holding a line between the Valasjärvi and Vaatsherjärvi where the Nikel Road meets the Arctic Ocean Highway. Jodl told Rüf that the position was integral to the defence of Kirkenes. Rüf had the Von Erfer Abteilung of Radfahr-Aufklärungs-Brigade Norwegen 6km south on the Tollevi Hill by Lake Kuotsi. Gebirgsjäger-Regiment 141 held the area north of Vaatscherjärvi. The I./Gebirgsjäger-Regiment 143 was on the road forward of that by the 235.5m-high Reutashaoivi. Rüf told Jodl that his companies were very weak, with only two *Leutnante* that had recently graduated. He was preparing to intervene personally in the battle because of the lack of officers. He expected close combat and rapid counter-attacks. He stressed the need for hand grenades. He expected tanks and bemoaned the lack of anti-tank weapons. Artillery was also lacking. Soon after this, a 7.5cm anti-tank unit and tank-busting soldiers arrived. Gebirgs-Artillerie-Regiment 118 also sent a forward observer. Soviet sources describe how tank units were unable to effectively support their advance here. German anti-tank guns on the road targeted them, and they were delayed by mines on the road and could only operate singly or in pairs.

At 1500 hrs on 21 October, I./Gebirgsjäger-Regiment 143 reported an enemy advance that forced them back to the Tollevi. Then the radio line failed. The battalion was cut off from reaching the road. One unit was caught between Valasjärvi and the road. A grenadier company on the other side of the lake 300–400m away failed to open fire to cover their withdrawal across the river; the company commander was court-martialled; his excuse was that he did not want to reveal his position to the enemy. The rest of I./Gebirgsjäger-Regiment 143 and the Radfahr unit reached Rüf's positions, but incurred heavy losses.

On 22 October, the Soviets attacked Rüf's unit. One *Gefreiter* had his MG34 malfunction. He grabbed a rock, and pretending it was a grenade, threw it at the Soviets. The attackers took cover and the *Gefreiter* withdrew behind to repair the weapon. Companies were at platoon strength and close to breaking point. The 6.Kompanie from II./Gebirgsjäger-Regiment 143 reinforced Rüf's unit just in time. Mortar fire was brought down within 50m of friendly positions. The Soviets had to go around the position further west and force Rüf to give up his position.

Only on the evening of 22 October did the Soviets reach the Norwegian border on the Pasvik River. On 23 October, two regiments of 114th Rifle Regiment crossed it, using improvised rafts and the US Lend-Lease amphibious jeeps of 284th Special Purpose Motorized Battalion. The 65th Rifle Division succeeded in crossing the Pasvik at Trangsund. That night, 96th Separate Motorized Pontoon Bridge Battalion, whilst being fired at by artillery, established a 250–275m floating pontoon over the Paatsjoki River at Holmfoss.

The 126th Light Rifle Corps, ordered to support 99th Rifle Corps on its northern flank, had provided limited support to the advance. They had received 51 tons of supplies after the first phase of the operation, but losses that brought them to the road junction west of Luostari were heavy. On 18 October, they moved along Tarnet Road and then veered off; in the following days, they moved 23km across difficult terrain, with 72nd Naval Rifle Brigade reaching Lake Klistervatn on 22 October having defeated Radfahr-Aufklärungs-Brigade Norwegen. They then moved to interdict the road from Akhmalakhti to Kirkenes. Isolated from 99th Rifle Corps, they had to stay on this road north of Lake Klistervatn until 23 October because of logistical issues.

The Nikel Road

On 18 October, the 1217th Rifle Regiment (belonging to Colonel A. Startsev's 367th Rifle Division) commanded by Major Mikhaylin advanced 6–7km and reached the eastern slopes of Hill 466. One battalion with Mayerov's tank company had advanced down the road whilst another infantry battalion carried out a flank march. The hill was defended by a battalion of Infanterie-Regiment 324 with guns from Artillerie-Regiment 234 in support; they forced the Soviet regiment to take cover and wait for their artillery to reach them. The two regiments of the division following were stacked behind. Lieutenant-General Shcherbakov thought the Germans would withdraw, and wanted Nikel captured by 19 October. Major-General Absaliamov, commander of 31st Rifle Corps, had laid out his forces for pursuit with only one regiment per division forward. Co-ordination and synchronization of assets was lacking,

On the evening of 16 October, 31st Rifle Corps began a long approach march. On the morning of 18 October, 367th Division made good progress before being brought to a halt in front of Hill 466. The 2nd Company of 89th Separate Tank Regiment, commanded by Captain V. I. Mayerov, formed the advance guard with a platoon of self-propelled guns and infantry, but could only advance on a one-tank frontage. (Courtesy of the Central Museum of the Armed Forces, Moscow via Stavka)

THE NIKEL ROAD: T-34/85 UNDER FIRE (PP. 76–77)

The German defensive by 16 October was concentrated on the Nikel axis. Here, 15,000 Germans would encounter 15,000 Soviets, but the Soviets had the advantage in artillery, deploying twice the number of guns. Off-road movement for vehicles was not an option. The road was the only clear path through and the Germans cratered the surface, laid barricades and planted mines. Defensive positions were sited to prevent the uninterrupted clearing of these obstacles and could interdict movement. On 18 October, the Soviet 367th Rifle Division advanced 6–7km and then was halted at Hill 466. The two regiments of the division following were stacked behind. The commander of 31st Rifle Corps, Major-General Absaliamov, had laid out his forces for pursuit with only one regiment per division forward. Soviet reconnaissance and intelligence assessments had failed to work out German intentions. Only one Soviet regiment attacked Hill 466 on 19 October, and the position was captured by the afternoon. However, Hill 441.4 further on soon halted the advance once again.

Soviet reconnaissance and observation by the morning of 20 October had established that the strongpoint on Hill 441.4 was fortified with a network of circular trenches, stone-reinforced machine-gun firing platforms, barbed-wire obstacles (both fence and concertina types) in 1–2 rows and minefields. The strongpoint dominated the road; its flanks to the north and south of the road were contiguous with untrafficable lake-swamp terrain.

Absaliamov, in the study he wrote after the war, blamed the terrain for restricting the ability of his forces to manoeuvre, and the strength of German defences. Also, the Germans could observe Soviet movements from dominating terrain. He reported that an engineer platoon supporting the attached tank brigade had to remove 452 mines and bombs in a 10km stretch, delaying tank support. Defences on Hill 441.4 were poorly reconnoitred and not effectively suppressed by artillery that had limited ammunition supply. Barbed wire was not identified and passages through were not made; engineer obstacles were effectively camouflaged in broken terrain. There were only 76 guns and mortars per kilometre of front, with firing carried out at grid references rather than specific identified targets. Poor communications precluded the use of 152mm guns that were available and the flanking forces had only 82mm mortars with limited rounds.

Here we see a T-34/85 (1) with Soviet troops in desant making its way along a clear portion of the Nikel Road. The tank is a Model 1945, with twin observation domes on the turret (2). A German position can be seen on the hill in the distance, some 400m away (3). The T-34/85 tank has been fired at, but not destroyed. The infantry riders are jumping off the halted tank. Most are wearing the *telogreika* padded jackets and trousers (4), and all have the distinctive *ushanka* fur caps (5). One soldier is wearing a great coat and is armed with a PPSh-41 (6). A sergeant, armed with a PPSh-43 (7), is already on the ground and is directing his men towards a small elevation.

especially with the air force. Soviet reconnaissance and intelligence assessments had failed to work out German intentions. Only 1217th Rifle Regiment attacked Hill 466 on 19 October; the position was captured by the afternoon, however, by 1800 hrs, positions on Hill 441.4 halted the advance once again. Here the Germans had built eight concrete dugouts, seven mortar-firing pits, 15 concrete-reinforced machine-gun emplacements, 1,200m of trenches and laid 2,200m of barbed-wire obstacles. The strongpoint was covered on every side by minefields, and on the flanks were lakes and swamp terrain. An attack on such a position required careful preparation, utilizing artillery for the destruction of the defensive fortifications and the suppression of the enemy forces, but the reconnaissance conducted in the evening was unable to reveal locations of the firing points and their system of fire.

The outflanking moves by battalions of the 1217st and 1219th regiments failed to threaten the German position on Hill 441.4, despite Mikulskii insisting that the commanders had the necessary maps. (TASS via Getty Images)

On the morning of 20 October, 1st Battalion of 1217th Rifle Regiment was sent north of the road and defeated a German force in the defile between the Kolosjoki River and Vyalikyampyanjärvi, and fought its way to the northern outskirts of Nikel. Here the battalion was subjected to heavy artillery and mortar bombardment, and later was thrown back to the area north-west of Vyalikyampyanjärvi. There it joined with 3rd Battalion, 1219th Rifle Regiment. This battalion had been sent by Colonel Startsov to attack Nikel from the north.

That same morning, Krautler reported that Hauptmann Rüf's 2.Schwadron of Aufklärungs-Abteilung 67 had approached Kaula Hill and heard the noise of fighting. The Soviets had already occupied the outer block huts on the road. They advanced in dense groups through the valley, and the Germans attacked them by rushing down the steep, bare slopes of the Kaula. Bombs from Soviet aircraft decimated their ranks, but the Germans closed with the Soviets and opened the road. Rüf was shot and seriously wounded by a Soviet soldier who had played dead. Haueisen sent his *Pionier* unit to help. Soldiers from Grenadier-Brigade 193 were brought in to reinforce the line. The appearance of Soviet forces on the northern outskirts of Nikel forced the German command to commit Gebirgsjäger-Regiment 137 too; however, 1st Battalion, 1217th Rifle Regiment was supposed to move on and influence the battle for Hill 441.4.

At 1000 hrs on 20 October, following a 15-minute artillery barrage, the 2nd and 3rd battalions, 1217th Rifle Regiment attacked Hill 441.4; however, encountering heavy artillery and machine-gun fire and impassable barbed-wire and explosive obstacles, they were forced to go to ground and subsequently withdrew to their starting positions. The barbed-wire and mine obstacles were inadequately reconnoitred prior to the assault. The attack was hampered because the artillery bombardment was restricted, with each gun having not many more than 10–12 rounds to fire. The 1st

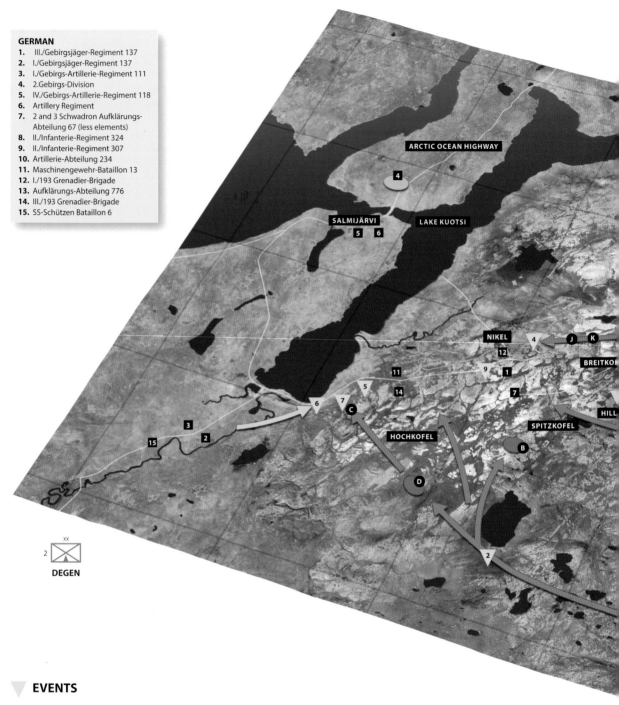

GERMAN
1.   III./Gebirgsjäger-Regiment 137
2.   I./Gebirgsjäger-Regiment 137
3.   I./Gebirgs-Artillerie-Regiment 111
4.   2.Gebirgs-Division
5.   IV./Gebirgs-Artillerie-Regiment 118
6.   Artillery Regiment
7.   2 and 3 Schwadron Aufklärungs-
     Abteilung 67 (less elements)
8.   II./Infanterie-Regiment 324
9.   II./Infanterie-Regiment 307
10. Artillerie-Abteilung 234
11. Maschinengewehr-Bataillon 13
12. I./193 Grenadier-Brigade
13. Aufklärungs-Abteilung 776
14. III./193 Grenadier-Brigade
15. SS-Schützen Bataillon 6

ARCTIC OCEAN HIGHWAY

SALMIJÄRVI

LAKE KUOTSI

NIKEL

BREITKO

HILL

SPITZKOFEL

HOCHKOFEL

2 XX DEGEN

▼ EVENTS

1.   Evening, 18 October: 127th Light Rifle Corps begins to transit the tundra.

2.   19 October: 70th Naval Rifle Brigade is detected by German aerial reconnaissance and is targeted by dive-bombers.

3.   19 October: 1217st Rifle Regiment from 367th Rifle Division, having captured Hill 466.3 with support from a company of the 89th Separate Tank Regiment, is halted at 1800 hrs before Hill 441.4 by II./Infanterie-Regiment 324. Its 1st Battalion is sent north of the road, where it joins with 3rd Battalion, 1219th Rifle Regiment.

4.   20 October: 367th Rifle Division has yet to neutralize German defensive positions on Hill 441.4. Other units from the division advance on Nikel from north and south of the road and reach closer to the town.

5.   1720 hrs, 20 October: The Germans discover the road is blocked 700m from the south-east corner of Lake Kuotsi. Elements of Aufklärungs-Abteilung 67 and III./Gebirgsjäger-Regiment 137 are surrounded.

6.   0800 hrs, 21 October: I./Gebirgsjäger-Regiment 137 forms up either side of the road near Lake Kuotsi, and supported by a heavy artillery bombardment attacks 3rd Battalion, 70th Naval Rifle Brigade defending a disused quarry near the road.

7.   1030 hrs, 21 October: 3rd Battalion, 70th Naval Rifle Brigade is destroyed. In total, 600 Soviet Naval riflemen are killed, 250 are taken prisoner and 150 escape. German troops around Nikel (1,000 men) withdraw.

8.   21 October: A regiment from the 83rd Rifle Division reinforces 367th Rifle Division; Hill 441.4 is captured, but German positions at Hill 482 stop the advance until 1900 hrs, when the Germans withdraw.

9.   Morning, 22 October: 127th Light Rifle Corps units move into Nikel from the south.

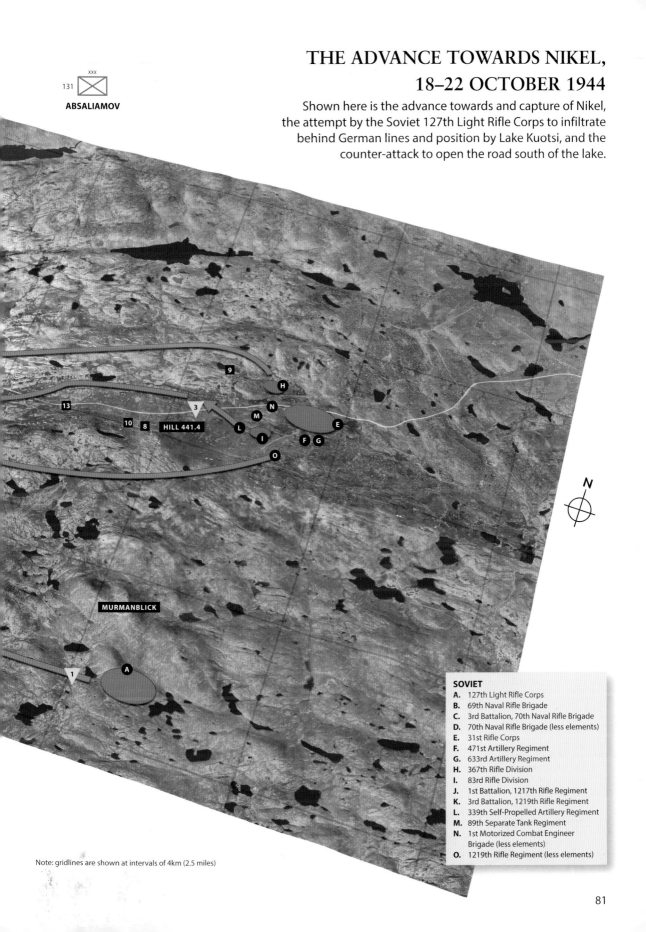

131 ⊠ XXX
ABSALIAMOV

THE ADVANCE TOWARDS NIKEL, 18–22 OCTOBER 1944

Shown here is the advance towards and capture of Nikel, the attempt by the Soviet 127th Light Rifle Corps to infiltrate behind German lines and position by Lake Kuotsi, and the counter-attack to open the road south of the lake.

9

H

13

3

N

M

10 · 8 · HILL 441.4

L

I

F G

E

O

N

MURMANBLICK

1

A

SOVIET

A. 127th Light Rifle Corps
B. 69th Naval Rifle Brigade
C. 3rd Battalion, 70th Naval Rifle Brigade
D. 70th Naval Rifle Brigade (less elements)
E. 31st Rifle Corps
F. 471st Artillery Regiment
G. 633rd Artillery Regiment
H. 367th Rifle Division
I. 83rd Rifle Division
J. 1st Battalion, 1217th Rifle Regiment
K. 3rd Battalion, 1219th Rifle Regiment
L. 339th Self-Propelled Artillery Regiment
M. 89th Separate Tank Regiment
N. 1st Motorized Combat Engineer Brigade (less elements)
O. 1219th Rifle Regiment (less elements)

Note: gridlines are shown at intervals of 4km (2.5 miles)

Battalion, 1217th Rifle Regiment was supposed to appear on the flank, but the unit, as already mentioned, met resistance and was unable to reach the flank of Hill 441.4. They were heavily counter-attacked, resulting in the wounding of their commander. The 1219th Rifle Regiment less its 3rd Battalion had gone south of the road during the day and should have attacked Hill 402, occupying the attention of German reserves, but it arrived late.

The attack of 1217th Rifle Regiment was done in isolation. The battalion commanders were unable and perhaps unwilling to recognize the absence of flanking units and did not delay their attack. Radio communication was not functioning. Wire communications only worked with interruptions. Orientation on the terrain especially at night was weak, and information regarding the location of units was imprecise. Absaliamov would assert later that many officers made the assumption that the Germans would withdraw and that careful battle preparation was less than necessary.

On the night of 20 October, after the failed attack on Hill 441.1, Lieutenant-General Shcherbakov, 14th Army commander, restated the importance of capturing Nikel and personally took charge of the preparations. Absaliamov would again use 367th Rifle Division to attack the hill, with 83rd Rifle Division preparing to follow; one regiment from this division was assigned to repair and improve the road, and another was sent to seize the airfield to the south of Nikel. Heavier artillery was brought forward, but 482nd Mortar Regiment only had 100 rounds to fire and 535th Guards Mortar Regiment had only 120. Multiple rocket launchers were also brought forward, but their targeting was imprecise. The 367th Rifle Division was not permitted to fire 76mm guns or 82mm mortars. The Germans withdrew from Hill 441.4 during the night; however, 1217th Regiment was unable to detect the movement, and only began its pursuit at 0730 hrs. The Germans retired to Hill 402.5, where Il-2 Shturmoviks and 1219th Rifle Regiment were brought in to attack them.

Crossing the tundra

The 127th Light Rifle Corps was ordered to capture Nikel. One brigade would attack Nikel from the south, whilst 70th Naval Rifle Brigade was ordered to cut the main road south-west of Nikel by 1700 hrs on 20 October. The brigade moved to jumping-off positions; in front was the reconnaissance company, behind it the brigade headquarters, then the submachine gunners; in the centre of the column were the 1st and 2nd battalions, behind them the artillery and mortars. The 3rd Battalion brought up the rear. The march was seen by a German reconnaissance aircraft, and on 17 October, during a clear night, whilst the brigade was in the vicinity

A German soldier in Lapland is checking to see if the aircraft flying above is enemy or friendly. A German Dornier is in fact approaching and the crew of the machine gun are not needed. (Martin Sachse/Ullstein Bild via Getty Images)

of Luostari Airfield, German bombers were heard. A bombing raid was launched that killed the political deputy commander of 2nd Battalion, Captain Rabinovich, and wounded the commander, Major Kalinin; in total, losses were 12 dead and 79 wounded. Kalinin was replaced by Captain G. Svetikov, the chief of staff. That night, low cloud cover prevented observation by enemy planes.

On the night of 18/19 October, 15km were covered and at 0900 hrs the following morning, in a desolate valley, German dive-

A German heavy gun prepares to fire in Lapland. German support of the attack to clear the Nikel Road from 3rd Battalion, 70th Naval Rifle Brigade was particularly effective. (Martin Sachse/Ullstein Bild via Getty Images)

bombers found them again. Thirteen casualties were suffered, and their presence was detected. Zhukov gave Sviridova's 3rd Battalion some mortars, but the mortars did not have much ammunition. Through frequent rain and strong winds and hail, the advance proceeded; the brigade column extended for 2km. The brigade encountered a boulder field and then a small swamp with stunted fir trees. Beyond the forest was an expanse of modest elevations, and the noises of battle were heard. The 1st Battalion had diverted off course and gone north. One platoon from 3rd Company was reduced to a handful of men when they were attacked on a hill. The rest of the brigade bypassed the hills and went into a swamp. Mortars and shells were fired at them, but landed harmlessly.

The Germans realized that the Soviets had sent troops to envelop their positions both north and south of the road. Degen, at the Gebirgsjäger-Regiment 137 command post, heard of this at 1615 hrs on 20 October, and motored to III./Gebirgsjäger-Regiment 137 at Nikel. Sviridova's battalion ambushed his car; Generalleutnant Degen narrowly escaped and reached Nikel. The I./Gebirgsjäger-Regiment 137, two Züge of the anti-tank company and the regimental mortar Zug were alerted. The naval infantry did not have heavy artillery, owing to the difficulties of the terrain over which they approached, but the probable presence of Soviet heavy mortars made artillery support particularly important to the German attack. On the morning of 21 October, the attack started. The Soviets, pressed on both sides, were soon encircled, and by 1030 hrs, resistance had ended. Some 600 Soviets were killed, the majority by artillery fire, and 250 surrendered. Around 150 men, separated from the main body and on patrols, escaped. The Germans lost 40 dead and 50 wounded. The III./Gebirgsjäger-Regiment 137, Aufklärungs-Abteilung 67 and the garrisons of the strongpoints withdrew into positions prepared by I./Gebirgsjäger-Regiment 137. Soviet naval riflemen entered Nikel at 0200 hrs on 22 October, and 367th Rifle Division moved in from the north-east at 0500 hrs. The largely uncommitted 83rd Rifle Division was due to exploit south-west down the road once the town was captured. The mines at Nikel were wrecked and the chimney stack destroyed. The bridges of Salmijärvi and Nordino were also destroyed. Dapra, from I./Gebirgsjäger-Regiment 137, crossed the Paatsjoki and secured the bank to stop the Soviets pursuing into Norwegian territory.

The 7th Guards Tank Brigade supported the 45th Rifle Division during its advance towards Kirkenes with mobile groups of tanks and tank riders going ahead of the infantry. (Sovfoto/UIG via Getty Images)

At 0500 hrs on 25 October, 14th Rifle Division attempted to cross Bekfjord at Elvenes. A 20-minute barrage was fired before the assault. The initial wave was driven back by strong German defensive fire. At 0600 hrs, there was another Soviet barrage, and the second attack succeeded in crossing. By 0900 hrs, 14th Rifle Division was starting to advance on Kirkenes from the south-east. (Courtesy of the Central Museum of the Armed Forces, Moscow via Stavka)

THE THIRD PHASE, 23 OCTOBER–5 NOVEMBER 1944

Kirkenes

Kirkenes was covered from the east by three fjords. Flanking these fjords were high chains of hills with steep slopes. The Germans had destroyed sections of the solitary main road, and built roadblocks covered by mines at passes. The 7th Guards Tank Brigade and 378th Guards Heavy Self-Propelled Artillery Regiment supported 45th Rifle Division in its approach to the town. Mobile groups with infantry on board the tanks went ahead of the main force. The company from 7th Guards Tank Brigade commanded by Captain N. Luchkin seized a crossing point over Jarfjorden ahead of the retreating Germans, and sank two boats. On the night of 23 October, 45th Rifle Division crossed Jarfjorden in amphibious jeeps and local fishing boats. On 24 October, there was little resistance as the division advanced to Jakobsnes across the fjord from Kirkenes. Tanks and multiple rocket launchers stayed on the south shore and supported 14th Rifle Division advancing to Bekfjord at Elvenes. Here the trestle bridge was already destroyed. Rafts were used to attempt a crossing on the morning of 25 October, but this failed. Two companies did succeed in crossing 1.5km south of Elvenes, on the second attempt, where the fjord was only 150–200m wide. From 23 to 24 October, German guns had fired 45,000 rounds at 131st Rifle Corps.

The 10th Guards Rifle Division had to cross a lake with amphibious vehicles before the approach on Kirkenes could start. Two regiments were brought over the pontoon bridge at Holmfoss on the night of 22/23 October. German artillery and mines along major routes through the woods hindered the pursuit. No artillery was available to the Soviet regiments, as the guns were on the other side of the lake. Air support was brought in at 1400 hrs on 23 October. Signal rockets and tracer bullets designated targets.

The attack was halted until 24 October, but the rocky, hilly terrain offered prospects for infiltration; by the evening, they were 16km south of Kirkenes.

A tank from 73rd Separate Guards Heavy Tank Regiment was hit going around a corner of the road and the regiment was held back. Artillery and mortars fired at the flanks and targets in depth. In the evening, Soviet air reconnaissance detected German forces moving out of Kirkenes along Highway 50 towards Neiden. Large explosions from the town indicated the Germans were destroying supplies stockpiled there. The 24th Guards Rifle Regiment followed the railway line into town. Tunnels provided good defensive positions, but by 0300 hrs on 25 October, the regiment and 35th Guards Rifle Regiment were entering Kirkenes. The defences on the western side of Jarfjorden were also ruptured, with 65th Rifle Division attacking on the right between the road and the Pasvik River. By 1130 hrs, the town was secure. A regiment of 10th Guards Rifle Division seized the airfield 15km from Kirkenes on 26 October.

The 28th Guards Rifle Regiment, in the second echelon, was detached on a 30km march to carry out 126th Light Rifle Corps' mission to the Munkelvn Road, which was being used by German forces to retreat from Kirkenes. The 126th Light Rifle Corps was halted because of lack of supplies. Large explosions from the town indicated the Germans were destroying supplies stockpiled there. Once the regiment went over height 250 that evening, the radio link with them was lost. A ski battalion commanded by Konoshenko was ordered to link with naval infantry and cut the retreat at Sandnes. By the morning of 26 October, the Munkelvn Road was cut. The town was captured that evening. This move prompted the Germans to retreat early, though it did not intercept their withdrawal. Konoshenko moved over the fjord and prepared ambush positions that did intercept some retreating units. Whilst this was occurring, 2nd and 3rd battalions of 63rd Naval Infantry Brigade landed at Holmengråfjorden, reaching Jakobsnes on 27 October, but this had no effect on the capture of Kirkenes.

The Neiden River was reached by 127th Light Rifle Corps on 27 October; German rear-guards delayed the river crossing momentarily. On 28 October, the offensive was halted. With winter approaching, and once Kirkenes was captured, there was little reason for the Soviets to continue their offensive. Rüf's unit was on a height between Munkfjord and Neiden River guarding the retreat of his division across the river. He thought the Soviets would cross a frozen marsh in the night and get behind his position, and voiced his concerns to the regiment commander. He was told to hold his position. Then, at midnight, 12.Kompanie reported movement; Jäger Figl had regained friendly lines and reported the presence of Soviet soldiers from the Light Rifle Corps moving behind them; this was enough to persuade the regimental commander that a withdrawal over the Neiden River was necessary. Once across, these Soviet soldiers were seen on the other side of the river with the break of day. The first units were wearing German uniform, but when reindeer were seen, Rüf realized they were enemy and ordered his men to open fire.

The Germans offered some resistance to the Soviet advance into Kirkenes as they were destroying installations in the town and evacuating the supplies that could be brought out in time. Here, a 45mm Soviet gun, which rifle regiments were provided with, fires from the ruins. (Courtesy of the Central Museum of the Armed Forces, Moscow via Stavka)

South towards Ivalo

The 31st Rifle Corps and 127th Light Rifle Corps received orders to advance down the Arctic Ocean Highway to pursue the Germans known to be retreating there. As the Germans had destroyed the roads in many locations, Major-General Absaliamov decided to launch flank attacks as well as frontal attacks. He realized the importance of attempting to keep the Germans off-balance and having artillery with the advance guard, but the road was torn apart by the Germans, and Soviet engineers were ordered to repair the road as the attack progressed. Again, the second echelon infantry

Kirkenes was the first Norwegian town to be liberated. The national flag is shown here being hoisted in October 1944. (SCANPIX/AFP/Getty Images)

Soviet soldiers rescue Norwegian civilians taking refuge in a railway tunnel in Kirkenes. (SCANPIX/AFP/Getty Images)

units were ordered to help the engineers. The commander of 83rd Rifle Division was told to have two regiments prepared to immediately begin off-road movement on trackless terrain without artillery or logistics units.

On 23 October, 70th Naval Rifle Brigade crossed the Shuonijoki River near the destroyed bridge and ascended the elevation on the other side where the road was blown up and the surrounding area mined; Pestanov reported how 1,000kg aviation bombs were laid in the road. In the evening, they reached the Norwegian border and had found captured provisions. They marched on the road that ran by the Pasvik River, but did not encounter any enemy.

At the bridge, the engineers had difficulties repairing it because the terrain either side was marshy. By the morning of 24 October, the engineer battalion of 367th Rifle Division was helping the engineers of 83rd Rifle Division, as were a battalion from 1st Motorized Engineer Brigade and two battalions from 46th Rifle Regiment of 83rd Rifle Division. Pontoon assets belonging to the engineer brigade were not available. Traffic could only start on the bridge and road on the morning of 25 October. Regimental artillery battalions, followed by the artillery regiment of 83rd Rifle Division, were the first to cross, then the Guards multiple rocket launcher regiment, a mortar regiment and then one battalion of 152mms guns. Tanks would not be used in the attack.

The divisional commander was with the lead regiment. On 24 October, 26th Rifle Regiment from 83rd Rifle Division was held up at Kaskama Hill, and experienced artillery fire from mortars and guns. Reconnaissance and observation established that, by the end of the day, a complex system of trenches and barbed-wire obstacles was along the northern and north-eastern slopes of Kaskama Hill; minefields were detected in places in front of the barbed wire, and particularly reinforced was the terrain by the road. Absaliamov ordered Colonel Nikandrov, the divisional commander, to carry out an outflanking move. Nikandrov was ordered to go to 26th Rifle Regiment with his operations staff and organize this move to cut off the Germans south of the Kaskama Hill. Nikandrov decided to launch a battalion frontally on the German defences and send two others around the flank to reach the road by the morning of 26 October. He was also bringing up 46th Rifle Regiment and some artillery for use by 26 October.

German sources described the road from Salmijärvi as being blocked by extensive mining and demolitions carried out with large-calibre bombs at suitable locations, for example Porojärvi and Maiatola. The road went through forest without any settlements and was good for any vehicle. On both sides of the road, the forest was interspersed with numerous

Nautsi: Phase 3 of the offensive

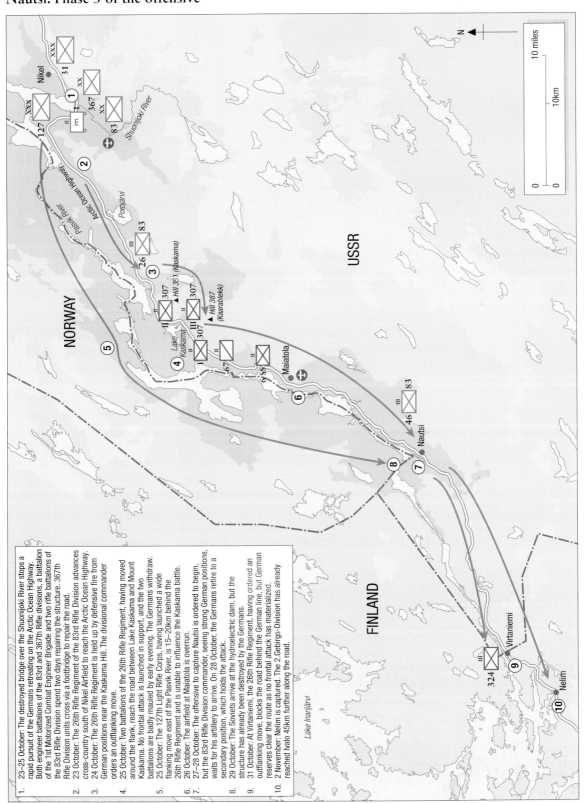

1. 23–25 October: The destroyed bridge over the Shuonijoki River stops a rapid pursuit of the Germans retreating on the Arctic Ocean Highway. Both engineer battalions of the 83rd and 367th Rifle divisions, a battalion of the 1st Motorized Combat Engineer Brigade and two rifle battalions of the 83rd Rifle Division spend two days repairing the structure. 367th Rifle Division units cross via a footbridge to repair the road.

2. 23 October: The 26th Rifle Regiment of the 83rd Rifle Division advances cross-country south of Nikel Airfield to reach the Arctic Ocean Highway.

3. 24 October: The 26th Rifle Regiment is held up by defensive fire from German positions near the Kaskama Hill. The divisional commander orders an outflanking move.

4. 25 October: Two battalions of the 26th Rifle Regiment, having moved around the flank, reach the road between Lake Kaskama and Mount Kaskama. No frontal attack is launched in support, and the two battalions are badly mauled by early evening. The Germans withdraw.

5. 25 October: The 127th Light Rifle Corps, having launched a wide flanking move east of the Pasvik River, is 15–20km behind the 26th Rifle Regiment and is unable to influence the Kaskama battle.

6. 26 October: The airfield at Maiatola is overrun.

7. 27–28 October: The offensive to capture Nautsi is ordered to begin, but the 83rd Rifle Division commander, seeing strong German positions, waits for his artillery to arrive. On 28 October, the Germans retire to a secondary position, which holds the attack.

8. 29 October: The Soviets arrive at the hydroelectric dam, but the structure has already been destroyed by the Germans.

9. 31 October: At Virtaniemi, the 26th Rifle Regiment, having ordered an outflanking move, blocks the road behind the German line, but German reserves clear the route as no frontal attack has materialized.

10. 2 November: Nelim is captured. The 2.Gebirgs-Division has already reached Ivalo 45km further along the road.

87

On 25 October, the advance of the artillery units had resumed, but there were significant shortages of ammunition. Quantities of 120mm mortar and 76mm and 122mm gun rounds were at between 20 and 30 per cent of what they were supposed to be. Rounds for 82mm mortars were at 40 per cent. Even though some guns were moved up by vehicular transport, combat units were unable to fight as effectively as they should have because of the scarce supply of ammunition (Nik Cornish at www.Stavka.org.uk)

lakes and many swamps and rivers. The road near Kaskama was flanked by steep elevations about 200m high. Near where the road went round Lake Kaskamajärvi, the height reached 357m. East of the road, the Kaskama and Kaarablekk hills were 351 and 387m high. The lower slopes (the first third elevation) were covered with stunted trees, but higher than this the slopes were bare and rocky. The weather was cold and clear with no snow. Daybreak was at 0900 hrs, with fog sometimes persisting to late morning.

Infanterie-Regiment 307 had built defensive positions to delay the Soviet pursuit at Kaskama. The unit placed one battalion on the Kaskama and Kaarablekk hills, with one company on each peak, reconnaissance detachments on the lower ridges to maintain contact and the third company on the western slope of the massif. Another battalion defended the road between Mount Kaskama and the lake, with one platoon occupying Hill 357. The I./Infanterie-Regiment 307 was in reserve between Nilijärvi and the road. German engineers were surprised that the Soviets were using the road by the evening of 24 October. Movement on the road suggested there would be an offensive the next day; however, the following morning infantry patrols accompanied by artillery spotting fire was the only enemy activity experienced to the front.

The more immediate worry was the appearance of a Soviet battalion on the road south of the Kaskama Hill. This unit had used the darkness and fog to infiltrate between the Kaskama and Kaarablekk hills and sit astride the road. Machine-gun and mortar fire from the Soviet battalion had created confusion, as the Germans on the peaks did not see and did not know what was taking place in the valley. The I./Infanterie-Regiment 307 attempted to counter-attack, but was forced onto the Kaskama massif. They needed help to clear the road, and when units from the front line were committed, the road was cleared by 1815 hrs, permitting the rearguard to withdraw. The Soviet battalion was driven off the road, but not destroyed.

At 1530 hrs on 25 October, 3rd Battalion, 26th Rifle Regiment had reached the road south-west of the Kaskama Hill. The 1st Battalion, 26th Rifle Regiment had bypassed the 3rd Battalion to the south, but because of the complexity of the terrain, the two battalions were unable to support each other. The German attack on 3rd Battalion had artillery support and was launched from south of Kaskama Hill.

The German commander commended the tenacity of the Soviet enveloping force, but noted that the main force was hesitant in attacking. The enveloping battalions had crossed trackless terrain with poor maps and carried more ammunition and less food. The occupation of the peaks by the German defenders was a mistake, as the Soviets could infiltrate between them. The German defenders were fortunate that co-operation between the enemy forces in the German rear and those in front was poor. A simultaneous attack by both would have resulted in heavy losses. Lack of radios, inflexibility in executing orders and lack of ability on the part of lower commanders to think independently was to blame.

Nikandrov prepared to attack on 26 October with artillery that had arrived late on 25 October. The German retreat was noticed, and by 0100 hrs on 26 October, Kaskama Hill was captured. Artillery was not needed and fell

Co-ordinating units in hilly terrain was difficult. The outflanking battalions of 83rd Rifle Division at Kaskama could not effectively support each other, and the frontal attack to relieve pressure on them did not materialize. (Nik Cornish at www.Stavka.org.uk)

increasingly behind during the pursuit because of the damage to the road. Absaliamov suggested that if 127th Light Rifle Corps had kept pace, the Germans would not have successfully withdrawn. He also suggested that poor reconnaissance of the routes of march movement and insufficient command/control of the regiment led to a situation where the battalions of the 26th Rifle Regiment, at the decisive moment of the fighting, were mired in swampy terrain and unable to conduct coordination, which permitted the enemy to break through with a portion of his forces. Nonetheless, the arrival of 26th Rifle Regiment into the enemy's rear and the skilful and decisive actions of its 3rd Battalion forced the Germans to abandon an exceptionally favourable position for defence and powerful strongpoint of resistance.

The 70th Naval Rifle Brigade was ordered to cross the swampy plain by the Paatsjoki River and force the river to interdict the German retreat. Wire found on the Nautsi highway was stretched along the column in order that the soldiers could stay in touch during the night march. Norwegian fishermen shipped the men across the River Paatsjoki. They reported that the Germans had already retreated. The locals supplied them with provisions from the border village of Stenbak. The road was reached, but several sections were potholed by land mines.

Infanterie-Regiment 307 was free to withdraw behind positions defended by Infanterie-Regiment 324 on the road 45km north-east of Ivalo in the Virtoniemi area. The road here went between several lakes to the east and the Paatsjoki River on the opposite side. Two battalions were holding the front with reserves in the village immediately behind them. Forward positions were 3km forward of this line near the road, a patrol was sent to the river and one battalion was in reserve 5km to the south-west at kilometre 345. Observers noticed movement on the morning of 31 October, but no attack materialized in front. Instead, an enveloping force, again sent through the forest, blocked the road behind the front. The reserve battalion launched a successful counter-attack. The enveloping force was too weak to do serious damage and too inflexible to withdraw, and was routed. When the Germans recommenced their retreat, the Soviets pursued to Ivalo, where they met up with Finnish troops on 5 November. In the campaign, the Germans had suffered nearly 9,000 casualties and the Soviets nearly 16,000.

AFTERMATH

By 24 October, with the protection of the Kriegsmarine's 4.Zerstörer-Flottille, the Germans evacuated Kirkenes relatively undisturbed. On 26 October, a Soviet destroyer flotilla was sent out on its only sortie to intercept German convoys, but was too late and carried out a desultory artillery duel with coastal batteries in Vardö. The larger battleship and cruiser available remained in port for the whole of October. Suprun (2007) suggests a verbal order directing Golovko not to risk the capital ships was given to him, and the loss or damage of major combatants was politically undesirable. The main aim of the navy – to interdict the evacuation by sea of German forces – failed. The Northern Fleet Air Force was more engaged. On 12 October alone, 200 sorties were made on German ships at sea and in Kirkenes. These attacks sank one transport, a destroyer escort, a minesweeper, an escort vessel, three escort cutters, two self-propelled barges, three motorized launches and one unidentified ship. Three transports and three motorized launches were damaged. A reconnaissance aircraft detected an enemy convoy in the Porsangerfjorden area at 0925 hrs on 14 October. It consisted of two large transports, two destroyer escorts, four escort vessels, five escort cutters and one minesweeper. Five torpedo-bombers sortied to attack the convoy. They sank both transports, with a combined displacement of 14,000 tons, and one enemy escort cutter in a sudden and bold attack. Air reconnaissance detected a large enemy convoy moving north from Kirkenes on the morning of 16 October. It contained three transports, two destroyer escorts, six escort vessels, a minesweeper, two self-propelled barges and 13 escort cutters. Three fighter aircraft flew air cover over the convoy. Northern Fleet Air Forces flew 116 sorties in five successive attacks on the convoy that day, but Soviet sources do not mention the results. Despite these earlier efforts, a third of German equipment and supplies were successfully withdrawn, mostly from Varanger Peninsula, on over 100 ships prior to the Soviets capturing Kirkenes.

The German retreat continued into northern Norway and ended 1,000km later on the Lyngen Line in January 1945. A scorched-earth policy was adopted in Finnish Lapland and Norway's Finnmark. Buildings were burnt down, road and rail lines destroyed, 43,000 people were deported and 130,000 mines and

On 24 October, Gebirgsjäger-Regiment 137 passed Nautsi Airfield and pioneers used aerial bombs to destroy the road. The power station at Jäniskoski was also destroyed. The dam was destroyed and water from Lake Inari poured over the flood plain of the Paatsjoki. On 28 October, they reached Ivalo, where I./Gebirgsjäger-Regiment 136, which had deployed away from the division in the autumn, joined them. The division marched to the north rather than the south, a detour of 1,000km, on the same path they had marched on in 1941, but at least there was respite from pursuit and time to recover. (Martin Sachse/Ullstein Bild via Getty Images)

other explosives planted. Generaloberst Rendulic carried out this order from Hitler, though Ferdinand Jodl thought such a policy was militarily unnecessary. The 2.Gebirgs-Division swung north-west into northern Norway and then transferred to the Western Front. The 6.Gebirgs-Division had an easier time because they stayed in Norway for the rest of the war and surrendered to the British in May 1945.

The Soviet Navy was unable or unwilling to interdict escaping German ships, preferring to rely on the Northern Fleet Air Force. Here, a German ship heads out through the Norwegian fjords in the northern Arctic. (Martin Sachse/Ullstein Bild via Getty Images)

CONCLUSION

The German defence of the Titovka River line enabled the retreat and escape of most of 2.Gebirgs-Division. Major-General Mikulskii's units were delayed in reaching the river, and he sought to explain this situation; he wrote how the army was not properly prepared for the offensive. They were only given two months to improve the road network. Roads to bring up vehicles for tanks or trucks bringing ammunition were not sufficient. His formation had to assemble in the area of front that 126th Light Rifle Corps had previously occupied; their defensive line did not support the reliable observation and reconnaissance of German positions. Guns and mortars were positioned a long way from the German line. Infantry could not move up to their jumping-off positions without being noticed. Guns that would support them by direct fire were only moved up the night before the offensive began. There was a long delay reaching the river in this area because the defences were not properly determined through reconnaissance and the use of other intelligence assets. Combat reconnaissance was not organized. Poor weather hampered reconnaissance sorties and bombing attacks by the air force. The 89th Separate Tank Regiment had not arrived in time to participate in the opening phase of the offensive, and was then held in reserve by the army commander. Despite the proliferation of artillery regiments, Mikulskii thought the artillery support was weak, with 95 guns and mortars per kilometre of front. He also complained that engineer support was limited, being the weakest part of the planning. He wrote that the engineers in their plan should have appreciated better the artillery's need to move forward their guns. The second echelon and reserves had to be deployed on road building because this was done badly; they could not be used to reinforce success or respond to German counter-attacks.

Interestingly, Mikulskii wrote that tactics to suppress the strongpoints differed according to unit commander's preference. Some preferred methodical frontal attacks, whilst others included flank attacks to bypass nodes of resistance. Artillery failed to prevent the strongpoints from prolonged resistance, and night attacks by infantry to capture them were not carried out. Defensive fortifications were so strong that even heavy artillery could not be used effectively on them. Guns had to stay in place for two days because of the poor road network; only larger-calibre guns with ranges of 15km and greater could be used from their original firing positions.

German positions were strongest on roads, but the Soviets did not have sufficient guns with the range to target the Lanweg or Nikel Road. Aviation was at times the only provider of firepower support, but the rocky nature of the soil often hampered its effectiveness. With limited artillery support and no tanks, Mikulskii's formations could only cover 3km per day; this increased to 8km during the pursuit. The importance of the roads often resulted in open or weakly defended flanks. Careful observation of the enemy and reconnaissance to determine his locations was needed to keep these secure. Co-ordination of units was done predominantly by radio on trackless terrain, with wire laid on the main roads. The movement of supplies on the few roads was not always organized efficiently. Their importance dominated the battle, and capturing them often had to be done by frontal attack. Outflanking forces were often delayed because of the terrain, and these frontal attacks had to be done in isolation. Operational-level outflanking operations were a characteristic of the terrain, but were not always effective, because the forces engaged on these manoeuvres did not have the heavy weapons necessary to hold their positions.

Despite Mikulskii's protestations in regard to the German strongpoint line, the Soviets deployed four divisions in their first echelon against a single German division defending a zone 15km wide that only had a regiment in forward positions in front of the river with another behind the river in reserve. Each German battalion was defending against a division; their ability to withstand the Soviet attacks and in the majority of cases to escape to fight another day shows the exceptional level of leadership among junior officers up to battalion level. Strachwitz at Isarlager, Neuburg on the Nialla Massiv and Rüf on Speer Road and the Arctic Ocean Highway deserve special attention for their handling of their units. Degen wanted to intervene and was often in the thick of the action.

The attempt to cut off the retreat of 6.Gebirgs-Division failed because the amphibious operation was launched too late. Meretskov did not want to wait to see if his ground attack was successful, and had asked Stavka to start the naval infantry operations concurrently with the army's offensive, but was vetoed. Moscow seemed wary and exerted tight control on amphibious operations of the Northern Fleet. Admiral I. V. Platanov, the head of the Northern Fleet's headquarters, gave another example of their caution. In his memoirs, he stated that following the capture of Petsamo, a landing was planned on the northern shore of Varangerfjord near Vadsö and Vardö in order to gain sea control of Varanger Bay; troops were loaded onto boats, but a message was received from the People's Commissar for the Navy in Moscow, Admiral N. G. Kuznetsov, cancelling the operation. Overall, during the course of the war, 113 amphibious assaults were carried out, in which over 330,000 personnel were landed, as well as 46 major reconnaissance operations. Landings were aimed at the enemy's rear and flanks, with the intention of distracting enemy forces, foiling his offensive operations and giving time for ground units to regroup. Later in the war, they helped breach enemy defences on the maritime flank, seized bridgeheads for offensive operations and captured enemy ports and bases, but during the Petsamo operation their use, although tactically ambitious, had limited strategic effect. The use of the rifle brigades for deep flanking marches, across difficult terrain dominated by rocky hills and interspersed with ravines and swampy depressions, to sit astride German lines of communication was also ambitious. Such operations shared many attributes with amphibious landings; both were hazardous and fraught with difficulty, and in the tundra were even more difficult – but, interestingly, were still attempted.

THE BATTLEFIELD TODAY

Kirkenes was completely rebuilt after the war, and the Andresgrotta bomb shelter in the town that the population used during the 320 Soviet air raids that destroyed many houses is still there and open to the public. The tunnel near the town where 3,500 residents of the region sought refuge in October 1944 is preserved. Some 50,000 of the 75,000 population of the area were forced to flee because of the German evacuation order that month; others defied the order, living in tents and caves during the winter. The infrastructure of the region and most buildings were destroyed. Kirkenes suffered during the 1990s when the iron ore mine was closed. Tourism, new mining ventures and emerging oil and gas industries have revived the town in more recent times.

Harder to access is the Pechenga (Petsamo) area across the border in Russia. Nikel mining has led to ecological problems in the area. The Pechenga River is unhygienic because of the mining operations in the river basin. South of Nikel, sulphur-dioxide emissions from the smelting operations have led to plant life being eradicated. Petsamo has lost out to Liinakhamari because of the port's importance to copper and nikel mining. Nearby the port, the emplacements and fortifications of the two *Heeres-Küsten-Batterien* are still visible; there are signs of the presence of the two *Marine-Küsten-Batterien* at the end of the fjord. Border-patrol boats are based at Liinakhamari.

There are fortifications visible in the hills on both sides of the Titovka River. In Liinakhamari, the buildings are mostly abandoned, with only 500 people out of what once was 20,000 in the late Soviet era living in the municipality. The 1930s hotel in Liinakhamari has been rebuilt, and is used by the border guards. The airfield at Luostari is abandoned. The fields nearby are used by tanks to train on. In the barracks near the airfield site there is a museum devoted to Yuri Gagarin, as he was once based at the airfield. The Holy Trifon Monsatery at Luostari was destroyed by a Soviet tank during the Petsamo offensive; however, the building has been rebuilt and is in use. In Kolosjoki (Nikel) there is a museum about World War II and the Soviet offensive to capture the town in October 1944. Shuonijoki Airfield is abandoned. Salmijärvi was completely destroyed by the Germans and not rebuilt by the Soviets. Visiting the border area near Nautsi is difficult without a special permit.

BIBLIOGRAPHY

Unpublished sources and official reports:

The Northern Fleet in the Operation for the Liberation of the Soviet Far North [The Petsamo–Kirkenes Operation] (7–31 October 1944), translated by Major J. F. Gebhardt, US Army, Retired. Moscow, Directorate of the Naval Press of the People's Commissariat of the Navy of the USSR, 1946

Intelligence Support to the Northern Fleet during the Great Patriotic War 1941–45, translated by Major J. F. Gebhardt, Retired. Moscow, Directorate of the Naval Press of the People's Commissariat of the Navy of the USSR, 1950

Germany, Heer, 2. Gebirgs-division [Germany, Army, 2d Mountain Division], Kriegestagebuch nr. 1 [War diary no. 1], microfilm series T-315, roll 109, NARA

Germany, Heer, Gebirgsjagerregiment 137 [Mountain Rifle Regiment 137], "Gefechtsbericht ueber die Kampfhandlungen am 7. u. 8.10.44 im Abschnitt Isar" [Combat report of the battle action on 7 and 8 October 1944 in Sector Isar], in Germany, 2d Mt Div, KTB 1, microfilm series T-315, roll 109, NARA

Jodl, Ferdinand, General. "Kursbericht uber die Kampfhandlungen im Petsamo und Varangerraum" [A short report regarding the combat actions in Petsamo and Varanger area]. Dated 5 November 1944. Microfilm series T-312, roll 1069, item 75034/1, NARA

Published sources:

Arshinevskiy, V. 'Tiazhelye tanki v Zapoliar'e' ['Heavy Tanks in the Polar Region'], in *Eto bylo na Krainem Severe [It Was in the Far North]*, pp. 225–30. Petrozavodsk, Izdatel'stvo 'Karelia', 1985

Barchenko-Emelianov, I. P., *Frontovye budnyi Rybach'ego [Days at the front on the Rubachii Peninsula]*, Murmansk: Knizhnoe lzdatel'stvo, 1984

Brockelmann, Klaus, and Roschmann, Hans, 'Small Unit Tactics, combats in Taiga and Tundra', *Foreign Military Studies no. MS P-060m*, Historical Division, US Army, Europe, 1952

Burgess, W. (ed.), *Inside Spetsnaz: Soviet Special Operations – A Critical Analysis*, Presidio Press, Novato, USA, 1990

Chirkova, Z. K. (ed.), *Eto bylo na Krainem Severe [It Was in the Far North]*, Murmansk, Knizhnoe Izdatel'stvo, 1965

Gebhardt, J., *The Petsamo-Kirkenes Operation: Soviet Breakthrough and Pursuit in the Arctic, October 1944 (Leavenworth papers no. 17)*, US Army Command and General Staff College, Leavenworth, USA

Golovko, A., *With The Red Fleet*, Putnam, New York, 1965

Kabanov, S., *Pole boiia-bereg [The Battlefield is the Shore]*, Voenizdat, Moscow, 1977

Kamalov, Kh. Kh., *Morskaia pekhota v boiakh za rodinu [Naval Infantry in Battles for the Motherland]*, Voenizdat, Moscow, 1966

Krautler, M., and Springenschmid, Karl, *Es War Ein Edelweiss*, Leopold Stocker Verlag, Graz and Stuttgart, 1962

Leonov, V. (trans. J. Gebhardt), *Blood on the Shores: Soviet Naval Commandos in World War II*, Annapolis, Naval Institute Press, 1993

Meretskov, K., *Serving the People*, Progress Publishers, Moscow, 1971

Mikulskii, S., and M. Absaliamov. *Nastupatel'nye boi 99-go i 31-go strelkovykh korpusov v Zapoliar'e (Oktiabr 1944) [Offensive battles of the 99th and 31st Rifle Corps in the polar region (October 1944)]*, Moscow, Voenizdat, 1959

Pestanov, S. A., *Soldaty morskoi pekhoty [Soldiers of the Naval Infantry]*, Karelia, Petrozavodsk, 1976

Ruef, Karl, *Gebirgsjager zwischen Kreta und Murmansk: Die Schicksale der 6. Gebirgsdivision: ein Gedenkbuch*, Leopold Stocker Verlag, Graz and Stuttgart, 1984

Rumiantsev, N., *Razgrom vraga v Zapolaire (1941–1944): Voenno istoricheskii ocherk [The Defeat of the Enemy in the Polar Region (1941–1944): A Military Historical Outline]* Voenizdat, Moscow, 1963

Sintsov, A. N., 'Shturm Krestovogo' ['The storming of Krestovyi'], in *Eto bylo na Krainem severe [It Was in the Far North]*, ed. Z. K. Chirkova, pp. 225–30, Murmansk, Knizhnoe lzdatel'stvo, 1965

Suprun, Mikhail, 'Operation West: The Role of the Northern Fleet and its Air Forces in the Liberation of the Russian Arctic, 1944', in *Journal of Slavic Military Studies*, Vol. 20, Issue 3, Taylor and Francis Online, 2007

Velichko, M. (trans. Major J. F. Gebhardt, US Army, Retired), *Dvazhdy Geroy Sovetskogo Soyuza V.N. Leonov [Twice Hero of the Soviet Union: V. N. Leonov]*, Moscow, Military Press of the Ministry of the Armed Forces of the USSR, 1948

INDEX

Figures in bold refer to illustrations.